Intelligent Business

Skills Book

Intermediate
Business English

Christine Johnson

Pearson Education Limited
Edinburgh Gate
Harlow
Essex CM20 2JE
England
and Associated Companies throughout the world.

www.pearsonelt.com

First published 2005
Seventh impression 2012

ISBN: 978-0-582-84688-3

Set in Economist Roman 10.5 / 12.5

Printed in China CTPSC/07

Acknowledgements
The publishers would like to thank the following people for their help in piloting and developing this course: Irene Barrall, UK; Richard Booker and Karen Ngeow, University of Hong Kong; Louise Bulloch, Intercom Language Services GmbH, Hamburg; Steve Bush, The British Institute Florence; William Cooley, Open Schools of Languages, Madrid; Peter Dunn, Groupe ESC Dijon, Bourgogne; Adolfo Escuder, EU Estudios Empresariales, University of Zaragoza; Wendy Farrar, Universitá Cattolica del Sacro Cuore, Piacenza; Andrew Hopgood, Linguarama, Hamburg; Ann-Marie Hadzima, Dept of Foreign Languages, National Taiwan University, Taiwan; Samuel C. M. Hsieh, English Department, Chinese Culture University, Taipei; Laura Lewin, ABS International, Buenos Aires; Maite Padrós, Universitat de Barcelona; Louise Pile, UK; Jolanta Korc-Migon, Warsaw; Giuliete Aymard Ramos Siqueira, Sao Paulo; Richmond Stroupe, World Language Center, Soka University, Tokyo; Michael Thompson, Centro Linguistico Università Commerciale L. Bocconi, Milan; Krisztina Tüll, Európai Nyelvek Stúdiója, Budapest.

The publishers are grateful to The Economist for permission to adapt copyright material on pages 28 (©2003) and 103 (©2004). All material copyright of The Economist Newspaper Limited. All rights reserved.

We are grateful to John Wiley & Sons, Inc for permission to reproduce an extract from The Power of Nice by Shapiro and Jankowski © 2001 John Wiley & Sons, Inc.

Photograph acknowledgements
Alamy/Imagestate p14, A. Jenny p36(tr), P. Doyle p36(tl), J. Greenberg p36(br); Associated Press/S. Kaestner p58; Corbis/B.Schild p11,W. Morgan p28, T. Pannell p30, E. Bock p36(bl), W. Hodges p38, A.Bolante/Handout/ Microsoft/Reuters p40, Darama pp56, 57; Getty Images/C. Hawkins p13, J.Silva p15, Z.Kaluzny p20, M. Rosenfeld p21, R. Lang p24, Ryanstock contents page (m), p34, H. Silton p 42, AJA Productions p43, B.Scott p44, S. Potter, p 48, F. Herholdt p52, D. lees p62, J. Feingersh contents page (b), p70, A. Nagelmann p73; Panos Pictures/Mark Henley p25; Photonica/ S.Edson contents page (t), p 6, R. Utsumi p62; Punchstock (RF) pp 10, 65, 66; Zefa/J. Feingersh p48, L. Williams p49.

Every effort has been made to trace the copyright holders and we apologise in advance for any unintentional omissions. We would be pleased to insert the appropriate acknowledgement in any subsequent edition of this publication.

Front cover images supplied by J. Feingersh (tr), D. lees (tm), Punchstock (RF) (tl).

Picture Research by Sally Cole.

Illustrated by John Bradley

Designed by Luke Kelly and Neil Straker Creative

Contents

Unit 1

Meet business partners

This unit will help you review key phrases for greetings new partners and introducing yourself. You can also learn expressions for checking information and explaining your job responsibilities. **Page 6.**

Unit 7

Brainstorm solutions

This unit will help you practice the language of brainstorming: making suggestions and responding. **Page 34.**

Unit 15

Celebrate Success

This unit will help you to review the language for concluding a deal: summing up, reviewing achievements and praising your partners. **Page 70.**

On the inside back cover of this book you will find an interactive CDROM with extra activities, audio files and clips from the **Intelligent Business Intermediate video**. There is also a reference section with grammar, culture notes and good business practice.

From the author

The *Intelligent Business Intermediate Skills Book* provides a practical approach to developing each of the core business skills: presentations, attending and leading meetings, negotiating, socialising and telephoning.

The book is for intermediate learners who are either already in work, or studying and preparing for a career in business.

How can the book be used?

The Skills Book provides all the components for a complete course. However, it can be also be used in conjunction with the *Intelligent Business Intermediate Coursebook*. Each Skills Book unit gives further practice of language introduced in the equivalent coursebook units. There is also an *Intelligent Business Intermediate Video* that shows the language and business skills common to both books in practice.

The Skills Book can be taught as a one-week intensive course of 30 contact hours; or, it can be used for classes that attend once or twice a week over a longer period. It is designed for groups of four to eight students, but can be adapted for use with larger groups, or with one-to-one students. (See *Intelligent Business Intermediate Teachers' Book* for guidelines.)

What is in the units?

Each unit contains three practical speaking tasks, which are designed to develop the skills you need to meet the objectives of the unit. After each task, you will have a short analysis session, which will help you to evaluate your performance. There is also a listening activity in each unit, which provides a model of key language and will also help you to develop your listening skills.

The section *What do you think?* gives you the chance to draw on your own experience of business and say what you think are the key factors for success. If you don't have any experience of work, you can refer to the *Good Business Practice* section at the back of the book. The culture notes will help you to find out more about other cultures and their approach to common business situations. You can draw up your own culture profile by completing the chart on page 82.

There are five writing units in the book which will give you practice in the kinds of writing that are essential to business: emails, memos, short reports, formal correspondence and minutes of meetings. You can go to the grammar reference for information about the main grammar points, and for exercises to help you practise each of the key points.

The integrated CDROM will give you extra practice activities to do on your own. You can practise listening to the dialogues from each unit and watch short extracts from the *Intelligent Business Intermediate Video*.

I hope you enjoy using this book and find it helpful in improving your English. Good luck!

Christine Johnson

Bookmap

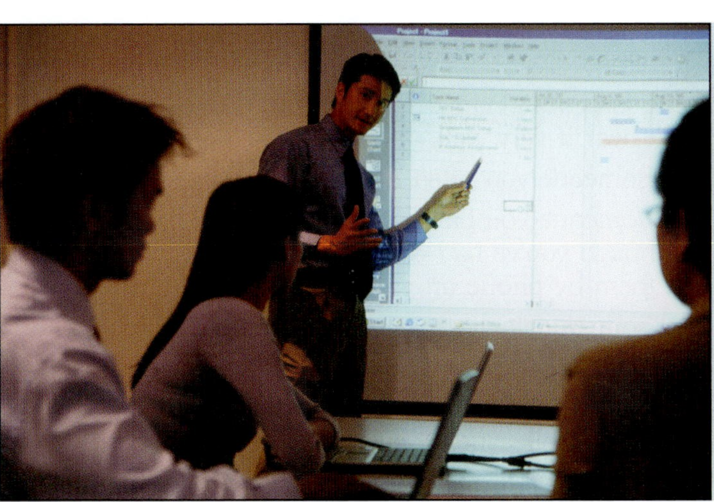

Unit 8

Get attention

This unit will help you to review language for presenting graphs and figures. You can study the language of change and listen to how English speakers stress key words when presenting. **Page 38.**

Unit 1 Meet business partners

| Introduce yourself | Talk about your job | Meet a new business partner |

Task 1
5 minutes

Objective: Introduce yourself

Walk round the room and try to talk to each person very briefly.

- Greet the other person and introduce yourself.
- Say where you work and what your job is.
- Find out the name, company and job of the other person.

What do you say?
10 minutes

Greetings and introductions

Read expressions a–h. They can all be used in the first few minutes of a meeting. Match them with the functions 1–8.

1 Greet someone you've never met before.
2 Check someone's name if you didn't hear it very well.
3 Greet someone you often meet.
4 Greet someone you haven't met though you've had contact with them by phone or email.
5 Greet someone you've met before, some time ago.
6 Introduce yourself.
7 Introduce a colleague.
8 Ask someone what their name is.

a Good to see you again!
b I'm Jan Davis, the Human Resources Manager.
c I'm sorry I didn't catch your name. Can you say it again?
d I'm sorry, I don't know your name.
e Hi! How are you?
f This is Carla Suarez. She's in charge of exports.
g Good morning. Pleased to meet you.
h Nice to meet you at last!

What other expressions do you know that match these functions?

Task 2
Pairs
20 minutes

Objective: Talk about your job

Take turns to ask the questions below. Answer your partner's questions as fully as you can. Be ready to tell the rest of the group something about your partner's job.

- Who do you work for?
- What type of company is that?
- What do you do in your job?
- What else does your job involve?
- What are you working on at the moment?

Try to use the following language when answering your partner's questions.
I work for ... *I'm in charge of / responsible for ...*
I report to ... *I manage ...* *My job involves ...*

Analysis
10 minutes

Did you understand your partner? Did you check understanding?
What can you tell the rest of the group about your partner?
Check that your partner gives an accurate report about you.

Grammar reference: Present tenses, page 83

Culture at work

Hierarchy

The way a company is organised depends on its culture: some companies have a ***steep hierarchy***, while others are ***flatter*** with a broader base. How would you describe your company culture? Complete your culture profile on page 82.

	Steep hierarchy ▲	Flat hierarchy ▲
Company structure	Many levels of management	Not many levels of management
Power	Unequal distribution of power: senior managers are very powerful	Power-sharing: members of staff are relatively equal
Roles	Each member of staff has a fixed role or function.	Roles are often flexible

What do you think?
Whole group
10 minutes

Meeting new business partners

What do you do when someone you haven't met before visits you in your office? In what order do you do these things? Mark your answers and then discuss your ideas with the rest of the group.

- ☐ Hand over your business card
- ☐ Shake hands with your visitor
- ☐ Greet the visitor with a formal greeting
- ☐ Introduce yourself
- ☐ Ask about their journey to your company
- ☐ Ask about your visitor's company and work
- ☐ Invite your visitor to sit down
- ☐ Be ready to meet your visitor at the appointed time
- ☐ Say good morning or good afternoon
- ☐ Offer something to drink
- ☐ Get down to business

Good business practice, page 80

CD 2 Listening
10 minutes

Paul Larousse works in an overseas subsidiary of Lisa Guzman's company. He is visiting head office for the first time for an international team meeting. Listen to the conversation and answer the questions.

1 Look again at the list above and identify the things Lisa did. Number them in order.

2 What expressions did Lisa use for:
   - apologising?
   - asking about Paul's journey?
   - inviting Paul to sit down?
   - offering something to drink?

Task 3
Pairs
2–5 minutes
per meeting

Objective: Meet a new business partner

In each situation below, a host receives a visitor from abroad. Take turns to play host and visitor. Before you start, decide which country each of you is from and in which country you are meeting. You can use real personal information or invent new identities. Act out the greetings and introductions, and if appropriate, make some general conversation, as in the listening activity. You don't have to discuss any business matters.

Situation 1

The visitor is from an overseas subsidiary and is visiting head office to meet counterparts in the accounts department. You have not met before but have communicated by email and phone.

Visitor: You arrive very late because your flight was delayed.

Situation 2

The host and visitor meet regularly once a month, usually for 1–2 hours.

Visitor: You are from head office. You travel a lot visiting the different subsidiaries and coordinating joint projects.

Host: You don't have the opportunity to travel much.

Situation 3

The host and visitor work for the same company. The last time you met was two years ago at a conference in Scotland. Since then, you have both been promoted to new positions in the company. You are going to start working together on a project.

Situation 4

The visitor and host are meeting to discuss an ongoing contract between your two companies. The visitor represents the supplier. You have not met before, but the host knows some of the visitor's colleagues in the export sales department.

Visitor: This is a new job for you, and it is your first time in the host's country.

Analysis
5 minutes

Describe what happened in the different meetings.
What did you talk about?
Did the host offer something to drink?
Was your partner polite? What should he / she say to be more polite?

Self-assessment

Think about your performance on the tasks. Were you able to:

- introduce yourself? ☐ yes ☐ need more practice
- talk about your job? ☐ yes ☐ need more practice
- meet a new business partner? ☐ yes ☐ need more practice

Unit 2 Get things done

| Talk about urgency | Persuade people to do things | Get things done on time |

What do you think?
5 minutes

Getting things done on time

Which of the following strategies do you use to make sure you do things on time?

- ☐ Make a list of things to do
- ☐ Estimate the time you need for each task
- ☐ Break down tasks into steps
- ☐ Decide on the order in which to complete tasks
- ☐ Draw a workflow diagram
- ☐ Put high priority tasks first
- ☐ Think about how to do things faster
- ☐ Other ideas ______________________

Good business practice, page 79

What do you say?
5 minutes

Talking about urgency

Which of the following sentences expresses the greatest priority? Put them in order from greatest to least priority.

a I'd like to get everything done before April, if possible.
b This is urgent – we must do it right away.
c It's important to confirm the numbers by the end of the month.
d We need to book as soon as possible.
e There's no rush – we can do that any time.

CD 3 Listening
10 minutes

1 **A sales manager talks to the conference organiser about arranging a golf tournament for important customers. Look at the list of actions a–g. Then listen to the conversation and write each action into the plan.**

a Check the customers' requirements
b Invite the customers
c Book the golf venue
d Brief the sales team
e Select the golf venue
f Choose the menu for lunch
g Confirm the number of guests

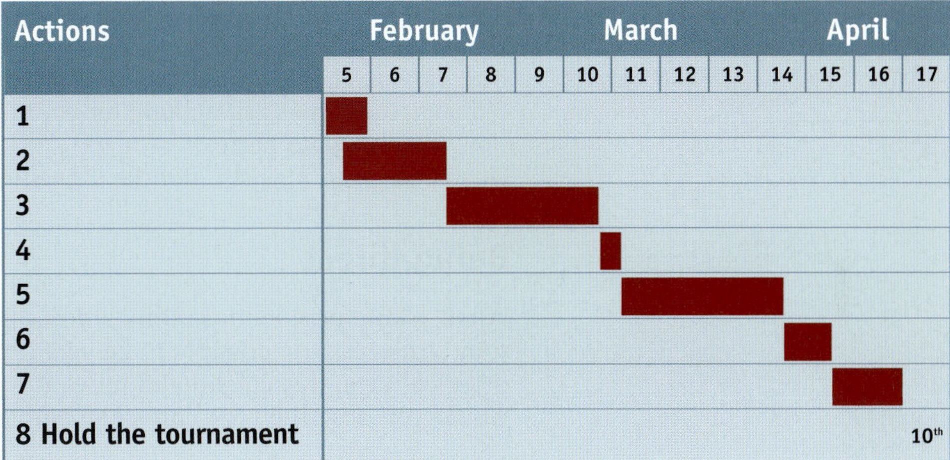

2 **Listen again. What language did the speakers use to say *when* things must be done?**

Task 1
Pairs
5 minutes

Objective: Talk about urgency

It is the end of February and actions 3 and 4 haven't been completed yet. Practise talking about the plan. Say what actions are urgent; say when you have to do them.

Task 2
Groups of 4
20–30 minutes

Objective: Persuade people to do things

Your team in Action Stations plc has a tight schedule tomorrow, but you each have to try to fit in one more task. Ask your colleagues if they can help. Use some of the following phrases to make polite requests.

Is there any way you can ... ?
I don't suppose you could ... ?
Would you do me a favour and ... ?
I wonder if you could ...
Would you mind ... (+ ing)?
I'd really appreciate it if you could ...

Role A turn to page 98.
Role B turn to page 100.
Role C turn to page 102.
Role D turn to page 104.

Grammar reference: Modal verbs, page 87

Analysis
5 minutes

How did you solve your scheduling problems?
Did your colleagues ask politely for your help?
How could they do better?
When you asked for help, did the others respond in a positive way?

Culture at work

Being direct

When asking people to do things, you can be either **direct** or **indirect**. In some cultures, it is possible to be very direct without being impolite. In other cultures, it is considered rude and aggressive to be too direct. How would you describe your culture? Complete your culture profile on page 82.

	Direct	Indirect
Form of request	Prefer to use the imperative: e.g. Send me your report this week, please.	Prefer question forms: e.g. Could you please send me your report this week?
Use of expressions	Make simple statements and use fewer words: e.g. I need those figures today.	Use more wordy expressions: e.g. I was wondering if you could let me have those figures today? It would really help if you could ...
Please and thank you	Use *please* and *thank you* less often.	Use *please* and *thank you* frequently.

Look at the following ways to make the same request. Which would you use to talk to a colleague?

very indirect
- I'm so sorry to trouble you. I wonder if you would mind getting me those figures?
- Do you think you could possibly get me those figures, please?
- Would you please get me those figures?
- Can you get me those figures?
- Get me those figures.

very direct

Task 3
Groups of 3–4
10 minutes per meeting

Objective: Get things done on time

Look at the projects below. Hold a short planning meeting with your team to discuss each one and make an action plan. Assign a different person to lead each discussion.

The leader's role:

- Get the team to break down each project into a series of steps or actions.
- Assign each action to someone in your team.
- Keep to the time limit.
- Record the decisions and actions on the form on page 101.

Project 1

Replace all the desks in your office.

Budget? | Requirements? | Suppliers? | Timescale?

Project 2

Organise a party for a colleague who is leaving in 2 weeks.

Time? | Food and drink? | Gifts? | Place?

Project 3

Organise a training day for your team next month. The trainer will come from the USA to run the course in-company.

Date? | Trainer's accommodation? | Training room? | Copies of training manual?

Analysis
5 minutes

Did each leader get the job done efficiently, politely and within the time limit? Was there anything they could have done better?

Self-assessment

Think about your performance on the tasks. Were you able to:

- talk about urgency?	☐ yes	☐ need more practice
- persuade people to do things?	☐ yes	☐ need more practice
- get things done on time?	☐ yes	☐ need more practice

Unit 3 Make a short presentation

| Prepare a short introduction | Sequence points and make a summary | Give a short presentation |

What do you think?
10 minutes

Giving presentations

Which of the following would you *definitely* want to include in a presentation, even a short presentation?

- ☐ some jokes
- ☐ your name
- ☐ details of your job
- ☐ visuals
- ☐ a summary
- ☐ the title or subject of your talk
- ☐ purpose: why the subject will interest your audience
- ☐ a 'menu' of main points that you will cover
- ☐ details of the background situation
- ☐ factual information, organised as main points

Good business practice, page 76

What do you say?
5 minutes

Structuring a presentation

Read phrases a–g. They can be used for organising and sequencing points in a presentation. At which step in the presentation would you use each phrase? Match phrases a–g with steps 1–7 in the framework on page 15.

a My second point is ...
b So first, I'm going to tell you about ...
c My objective is to ...
d Now let me summarise the main points again.
e The subject of my presentation is ...
f I've divided my talk into three parts. First, ... Second, ... And third, ...
g Now I'll come to my last point.

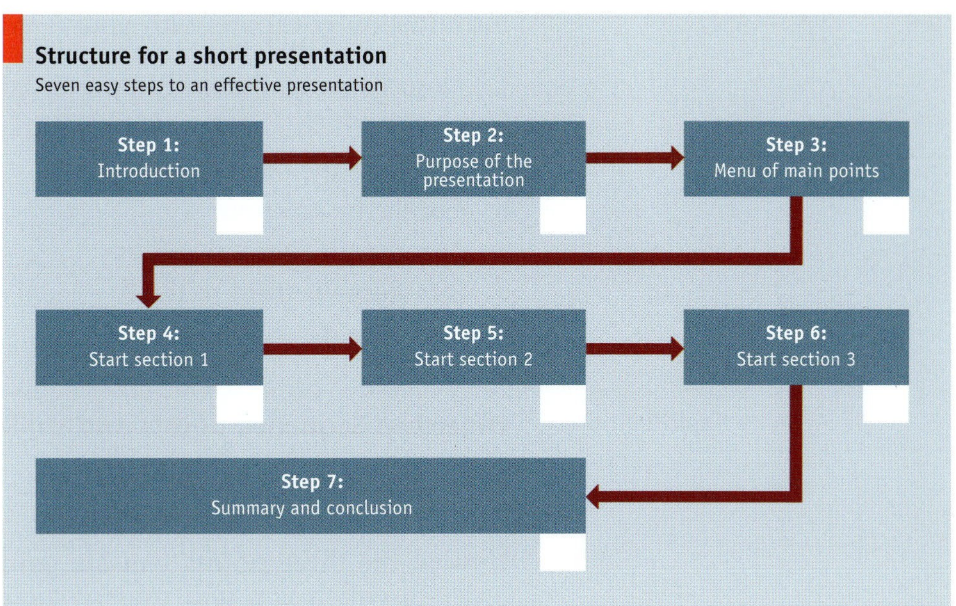

Task 1
Pairs
15 minutes

Objective: Prepare a short introduction

A Finnish construction company, AYT, is hoping to win a contract to build an apartment block in Poland. Leena Perttonen, AYT's marketing manager, will have three minutes to present an overview of AYT and its strengths to the Polish developers. Leena's presentation will cover the following three main areas:

1 General information about the company
2 International experience
3 Reasons for AYT's success

Step 1 Preparation

Prepare a short introduction for Leena and present it to the rest of the group. You should consider the following questions when preparing the introduction.

1 How should Leena introduce herself?
2 What is the subject of the presentation?
3 What is her purpose in making this presentation to this audience?
4 What is the 'menu' of main points that she will include?

Step 2 Presentation

Now present your introduction to the rest of the group.

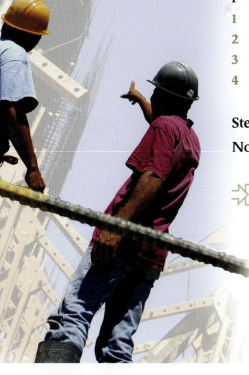

Grammar reference: Future forms, page 84

CD 4 Listening 1
10 minutes

1 Listen to the first part of Leena's presentation. How did her introduction compare with yours? What was similar / different?

CD 5

2 Now listen to the whole presentation. What expressions did Leena use to:

a introduce the first section? ________________

b end the first section? ________________

c introduce the second section? ________________

d introduce the third section? ________________

e introduce the summing up? ________________

Task 2
Pairs

Objective: Sequence points and make a summary

Partner A: Look at Presentation A.
Partner B: Look at Presentation B.

Look at the three points you are going to cover. Think about the order in which you will present these points.

Presentation A: You are presenting your company to a group of potential investors.

Main points:

- Our strategic objectives and plans for future growth
- Company history – reasons for our success
- Financial performance

Presentation B: You are presenting your marketing plans to a joint venture partner.

Main points:

- Plans for breaking into future markets
- Current markets and market shares
- Overview of company activities and products

Pairs
5 minutes

Step 1 Practise

With your partner, practise introducing and ending each section in the sequence you have chosen. Try to use some of the expressions from either 'What do you say?' or from the Listening.

Example: First, I'm going to give you some general information about the company.

So that was something about the company. Now I'll move on to ...

Pairs
5 minutes

Step 2 Summarise

With your partner, make a summary of the main points of your presentation. Use a suitable expression to introduce your summary.

Culture at work

Attitudes to time

Some cultures place a lot of importance on ***precise timing***. Other cultures feel that the timing of an activity should be ***approximate*** only. These different attitudes can affect the way people give presentations. How would you describe your culture? Complete your culture profile on page 82.

	Precise timing	Approximate timing
Timing	Presenters plan their presentation to fit the time available. They expect to start and finish at a precise time.	The timing is flexible and changes to the schedule can be tolerated.
Structure	Presentations have a tight structure with an introduction, a sequence of points and a summary.	Presenters prepare a rough outline, but often make changes as they deliver the talk.
Sequencing	Presenters move from one section to the next in a specific order.	Presenters may move back and forth between sections or points.
Following the plan	Presenters follow the plan exactly and often time each section of the presentation precisely.	Presenters are more spontaneous, responding to the situation and audience interest.

Task 3
Individually
10 minutes

Objective: Give a short presentation

Step 1 Preparation

Prepare a 3-minute presentation giving an overview of your own company, or one part of your company. You may include the following points:

- General information (activities, size, location)
- Products / markets
- Future plans

Use the framework on page 15 to organise your points.

Whole group
3 minutes
per presenter

Step 2 Presentation

Give your presentation to the rest of the group.

Analysis
2 minutes
per presentation

Was the presentation clear?
Were the introduction and summary effective?
How well did the speaker organise and structure the main points?

Self-assessment

Think about your performance on the tasks. Were you able to:

- prepare a short introduction? ☐ yes ☐ need more practice
- sequence points and make a summary? ☐ yes ☐ need more practice
- give a short presentation? ☐ yes ☐ need more practice

Writing 1 Informal emails

Get things done politely | Sequence the points in your message

What do you think?

1 If you want someone to help you, is it better to be strong or to be polite? Which of the emails below is more polite? Which email is better if you are:

- ☐ writing to a close colleague?
- ☐ writing to someone in another company?
- ☐ the boss?
- ☐ writing to someone you don't know well?

Email A

Email B

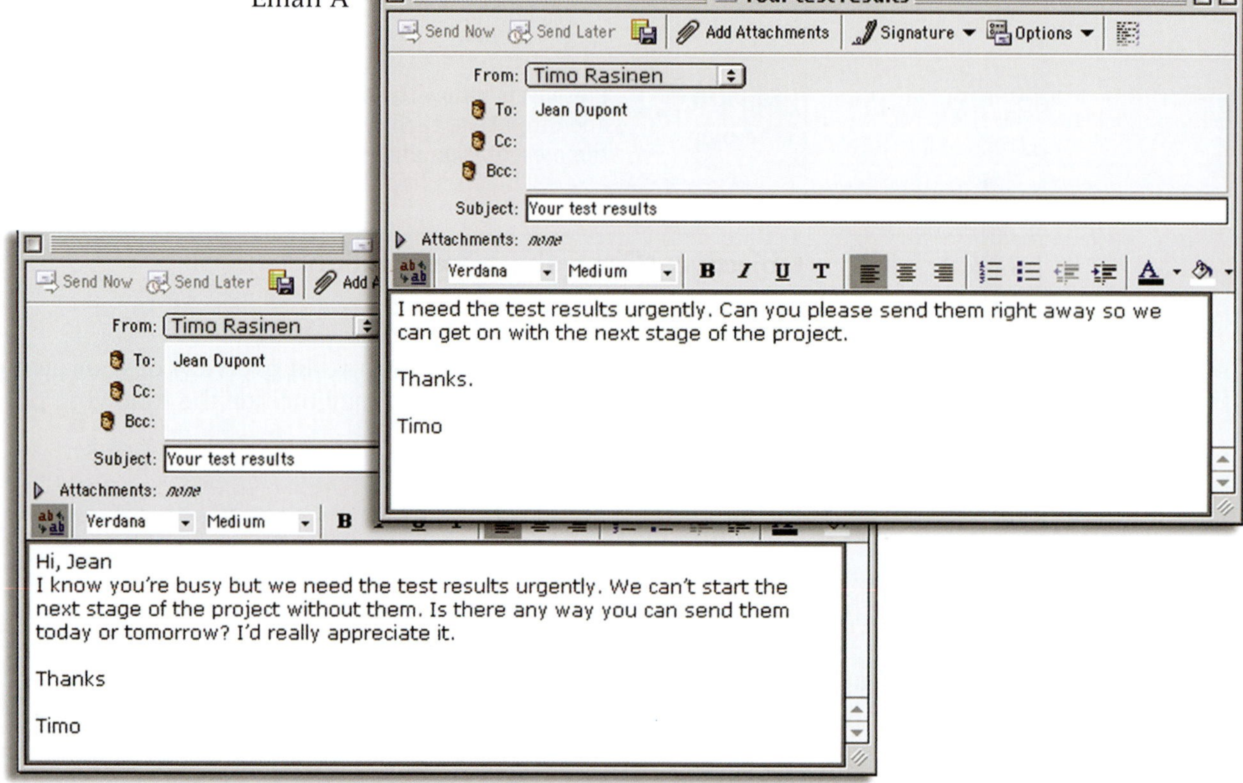

2 Underline the phrases which make email B more polite.

Task 1

Objective: Get things done politely

You have a new job as assistant accountant in a large company. At the end of the quarter, the different divisions send their figures to you to be consolidated. It is the last day of the quarter and you are still waiting for the figures from the northeast division. You need them by tomorrow at the latest. Send an email to Hella Hudsen asking for the figures. As Hella doesn't know you, you should start by introducing yourself.

What do you think?

1 **Most people receive a lot of emails each day. They want to be able to read and understand your message quickly. Look at these hints for making an email easier to read. Put them in order of importance.**

- Keep the message short.
- Write simple sentences.
- Put the main message near the start.
- Put important requests in the first paragraph.
- Use polite phrases to build a good relationship with the other person.

What do you write?

2 **Jacqui Bond wrote an email to Ili Enache about a meeting next week. The points from the message have been mixed up. Look at the recommended sequence of points below. Then order the message appropriately.**

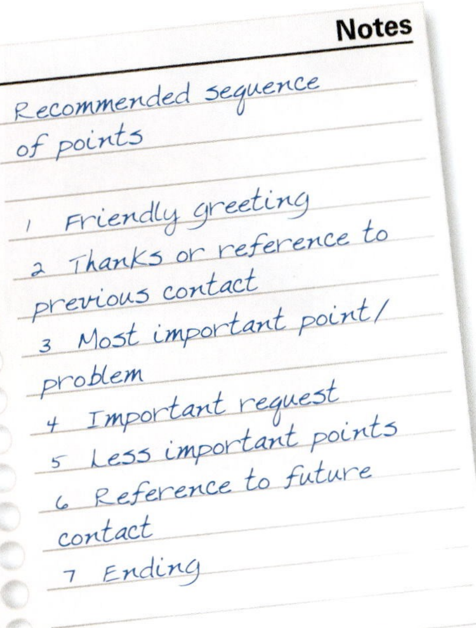

Notes
Recommended sequence of points
1 Friendly greeting
2 Thanks or reference to previous contact
3 Most important point/problem
4 Important request
5 Less important points
6 Reference to future contact
7 Ending

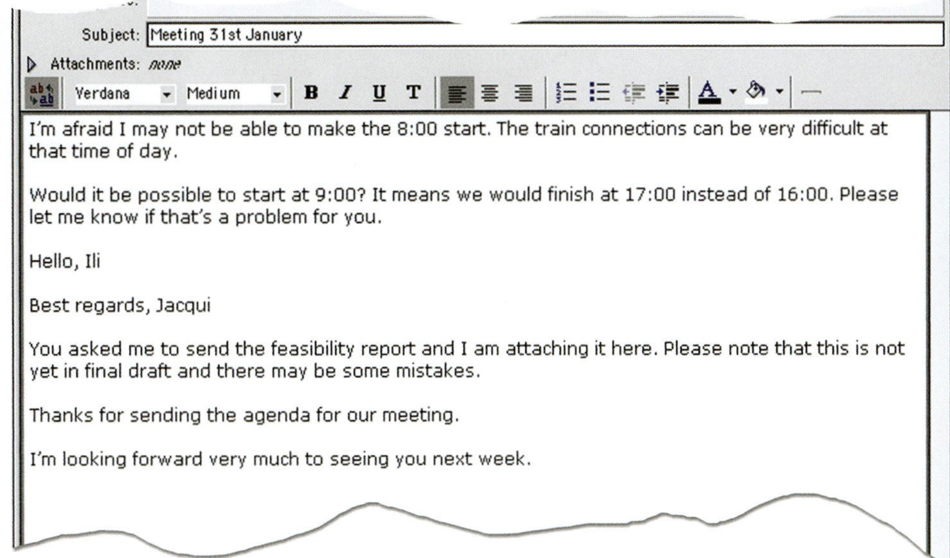

I'm afraid I may not be able to make the 8:00 start. The train connections can be very difficult at that time of day.

Would it be possible to start at 9:00? It means we would finish at 17:00 instead of 16:00. Please let me know if that's a problem for you.

Hello, Ili

Best regards, Jacqui

You asked me to send the feasibility report and I am attaching it here. Please note that this is not yet in final draft and there may be some mistakes.

Thanks for sending the agenda for our meeting.

I'm looking forward very much to seeing you next week.

Task 2

Objective: Sequence the points in your message

You are Ili Enache. Write a reply to Jacqui. Say that you can start at 9:00 but you will have to finish at 16:00 because you have another appointment after that. Suggest that you take a shorter lunch break so you can finish earlier. Don't forget to thank Jacqui for the report.

Sequence your points in the recommended way.

Grammar reference: Articles, page 94

Unit 4 Achieve objectives

| Set objectives | Open a meeting | Evaluate performance |

What do you think?
Whole group brainstorm
5 minutes

Setting objectives for meetings

Every meeting, whether it is for just two people or for ten or fifty people, has to have a clear purpose. Below are two examples of *purposes*, or reasons, for holding meetings. What others can you think of?

- give or share information
- present a proposal for discussion
- ______________________
- ______________________
- ______________________
- ______________________
- ______________________

CD 6 Listening
5 minutes

1 **An HR director introduces a meeting with other members of the HR team about a new performance-related pay system for the company. Listen for the answer to this question.**

What is the purpose of this morning's meeting?

Good business practice, page 78

CD 6
5 minutes

2 **Read the following five steps that leaders typically take when opening a meeting. Listen to the HR director again. Write the phrases he uses to introduce each step.**

Steps

1 Interrupt social conversation and signal the start of the meeting.
2 Greet and welcome participants; introduce new participants.
3 Explain the background to the meeting.
4 State the purpose of the meeting.
5 Ask for contributions or hand over to the first speaker.

Phrases

Step 1 ______________________________

Step 2 ______________________________

Step 3 ______________________________

Step 4 ______________________________

Step 5 ______________________________

What do you say?
5 minutes

Opening meetings

Look at some alternative language you can use to open a meeting. Match the phrases a–e with steps 1–5 above.

a John – could you start by reminding us what the three ideas were?
b Good morning, everybody. Thanks for coming along this morning.
c So the purpose of this meeting is to review the feedback.
d As you know, we've set up this team so that we can discuss ways of increasing staff motivation. At our first meeting last month, we came up with three new ideas, and we agreed we would all try to get some feedback from our colleagues.
e OK – Let's make a start!

Culture at work

Fixed objectives or flexibility?

When working on a project or business venture with other people, the partners have to find a way of working that will help them succeed. Some cultures like to define the task and specify their goals from the very beginning. Others are happy to let things develop as they go along. How would you describe your culture? Complete your culture profile on page 82.

	Fixed objectives	Flexible working
Objectives	People specify the objectives at the start of a project.	It is important to build a close relationship first. The partners can develop their objectives as they get to know each other.
Communication style	It is usual to explain everything in detail, write everything down and refer to the objectives often.	It isn't necessary to give detailed explanations because the partners understand each other: people are less specific and more flexible.
Evaluation	Partners evaluate the project on the basis of whether they have achieved the agreed objectives.	Partners evaluate the project on the basis of whether everybody is satisfied.

Task 1
Groups of 3–5
10 minutes

Objective: Set objectives

Step 1 Preparation

Read the problem below. In Task 2 you will discuss the problem and decide how to share the money. First of all, set some objectives so you can run an efficient meeting in Task 2. For example, you should decide on the following.

- Time: You only have 15 minutes for this meeting. (Is it your objective to make a firm decision in this time?)
- Organisation: (To give each person a chance to speak? To encourage free discussion? To keep it short by limiting discussion?)
- How to reach a decision: To have a consensus of ... per cent (e.g. 100%, 80%)

Problem

Your team has completed a highly successful project, and the company's directors have decided to give a financial reward of $10,000 to be shared among you. You have to agree how you want to use the money.

In addition, each individual should set a personal objective, such as winning over the others with your idea or making a strong contribution.

Step 2 Presentation

Now report your objectives.

Choose one person in your group to report the objectives you set, using appropriate language. For example,

We've agreed on three objectives. First, to ...
The main objective is to ...

Each individual should report his /her personal objective.

I've decided that my personal objective is to ...

Grammar reference: Present perfect and Past simple, page 85

Task 2

Objective: Open a meeting

Pairs
5 minutes

Step 1 Preparation

Plan how you will open the meeting to discuss the financial reward and what you will say to introduce each of the five steps on page 21.

Whole group
5 minutes

Step 2 Open the meeting

In pairs, demonstrate how you would open the meeting.

Analysis
5 minutes

How did each pair perform?
Did they include all five steps?
Did they make the purpose of the meeting clear?

Same groups as Task 1
15 minutes

Step 3 Hold the meeting

Choose a role. Read your role card and role-play the meeting. Start the meeting as soon as you can. Remember the objectives you prepared for yourselves in Task 1.

Role A turn to page 98.
Role B turn to page 100.
Role C turn to page 102.
Role D (groups of 4 or 5 only) turn to page 102.
Role E (groups of 5 only) turn to page 104.

Task 3
Same groups
10 minutes

Objective: Evaluate performance

As a group, discuss whether you achieved the objectives you set in Task 1. How did you achieve them? If not, why not? Ask each group member the same questions about their personal objective.

We managed to achieve our objective to ...
We had problems with ... because ...
It wasn't easy, but ...

Self-assessment

Think about your performance on the tasks. Were you able to:

- set objectives? ☐ yes ☐ need more practice
- open a meeting? ☐ yes ☐ need more practice
- evaluate performance? ☐ yes ☐ need more practice

Unit 5 Deal with problems

| Explain and clarify a problem | Predict consequences | Suggest and promise action |

What do you think?
Pairs
10 minutes

Telephoning problems

Read the typical telephoning problems 1–6. How would you deal with them? Discuss the strategies you might use. Then choose any expressions a–j that might help you.

1 You didn't hear the caller's name.
2 The other person speaks very fast and it's hard to understand.
3 The line is bad /your mobile phone signal is weak.
4 The caller is through to the wrong person or wrong department.
5 It is difficult to explain complex things on the phone.
6 The other person is asking for information you don't have in front of you.

a Can you say that again slowly, please?
b I'm afraid I can't help you with that.
c Can you spell that, please?
d Just hold on a moment, please.
e Could I send you the details by email /fax?
f Can I call you back?
g I'm afraid I can't hear you very well.
h I think you have the wrong number.
i Sorry, I didn't catch that.
j Just a moment. I'll transfer you (to ...)

Good business practice, page 80

CD 7 Listening
Pairs
20 minutes

A Canadian power company is about to start construction on a hydroelectric dam in Africa. The dam will flood 50km² of farmland and forest. Dan (project coordinator at the Vancouver office) receives a phone call from Robert (in charge of the project in Africa).

1 Listen to the first three sentences of the phone conversation and answer the questions.

a How does Robert ask for Dan McGuire?
b What does Dan reply?
c How does Robert introduce himself?

2 Now listen to the whole of the phone conversation. Listen once only and go to Task 1.

Task 1
Pairs
15 minutes

Objective: Explain and clarify a problem

Step 1 Explain the problem

With a partner, see if you can explain the problem with the dam in your own words. If there are some parts you didn't understand, what questions could you ask to clarify the situation?

Step 2 Clarify the problem

Put your questions to the rest of the group to see if they can answer them.

What do you say?
5 minutes

Dealing with problems

Match the expressions a–j with one or more of the functions 1–5.

1	Introduce the problem	a	Perhaps we could talk to them.
2	Ask for clarification	b	That'll result in even more expense.
3	Predict the consequences	c	I'll get back to you soon as I can.
	(4 answers)	d	Couldn't we bring in some people?
4	Suggest possible actions	e	How do you mean exactly?
	(2 answers)	f	It could be very dangerous.
5	Promise action	g	I'm afraid we've got a problem.
	(2 answers)	h	I'm going to call a crisis meeting.
		i	It'll mean lengthy negotiations.
		j	It might turn violent.

Culture at work

Dealing with unclear situations

Some cultures try to avoid unclear situations, but others can tolerate a lack of certainty. How would you describe your culture? Complete your culture profile on page 82.

	Avoid unclear situations	Tolerate unclear situations
Rules	Prefer to work with fixed rules and procedures	Prefer to have flexible ways of working
Precautions	Predict future problems and take precautions against them	Don't take many precautions and react when problems arise
Strategies	Find out as much as possible by asking questions or researching different sources	Are happy to wait and see how future situations will develop

What was Dan's strategy when responding to the problem in Africa?

Task 2
Pairs
20 minutes

Objective: Predict consequences

Step 1 Preparation

Read the problem, look at your role brief and then discuss the consequences of the situation.

Problem
Alex, a manager with YUS, is flying to Barcelona for an important meeting with a customer, XPorta. Jo, a colleague from the Spanish subsidiary of YUS, will also be at the meeting. Alex hopes to sign a big contract with XPorta. The ticket and email below explain the plan for the trip.

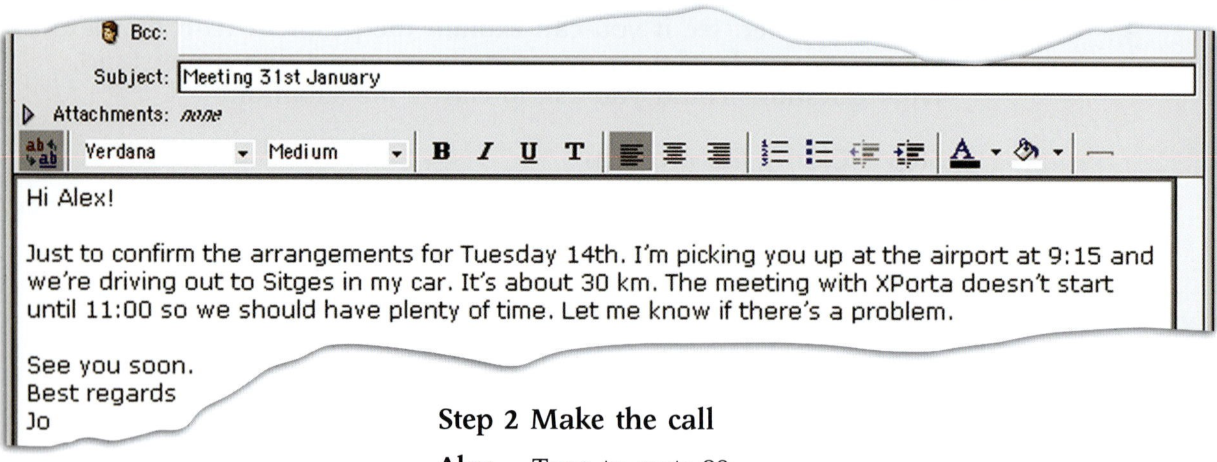

Bcc:
Subject: Meeting 31st January
Attachments: none
Verdana
Medium
Hi Alex!
Just to confirm the arrangements for Tuesday 14th. I'm picking you up at the airport at 9:15 and we're driving out to Sitges in my car. It's about 30 km. The meeting with XPorta doesn't start until 11:00 so we should have plenty of time. Let me know if there's a problem.
See you soon.
Best regards
Jo

Step 2 Make the call

Alex Turn to page 98.

Jo It's now 8 am on Tuesday 14th. You are in your office. You receive a phone call from Alex. Make sure you understand the problem.

Analysis
Who;e group
5 minutes

How well did your partner explain or clarify the problem?
What consequences did you each predict?
Did your partner use appropriate language for the telephone?

Grammar reference: Modal verbs, part 1, page 87

Task 3
Pairs
20 minutes

Objective: Suggest and promise action

Read the problem, look at your role brief and then role-play another telephone conversation. This time you should talk about possible actions. Each of you should promise some kind of action. If you took the role of Alex in task 2, take the role of Charlie.

Problem

Charlie works in the sales department, selling machine components. Your customer (Makers Ltd) needs a specific component today to repair a machine that has broken down. Production at the customer's company will be halted until the machine can be repaired, so they need the component urgently. Charlie has organised special delivery by van. The email to Boris Hanson gives details of the order.

Eddy Turn to page 100.

Charlie It is now 14:00 and you receive a phone call.

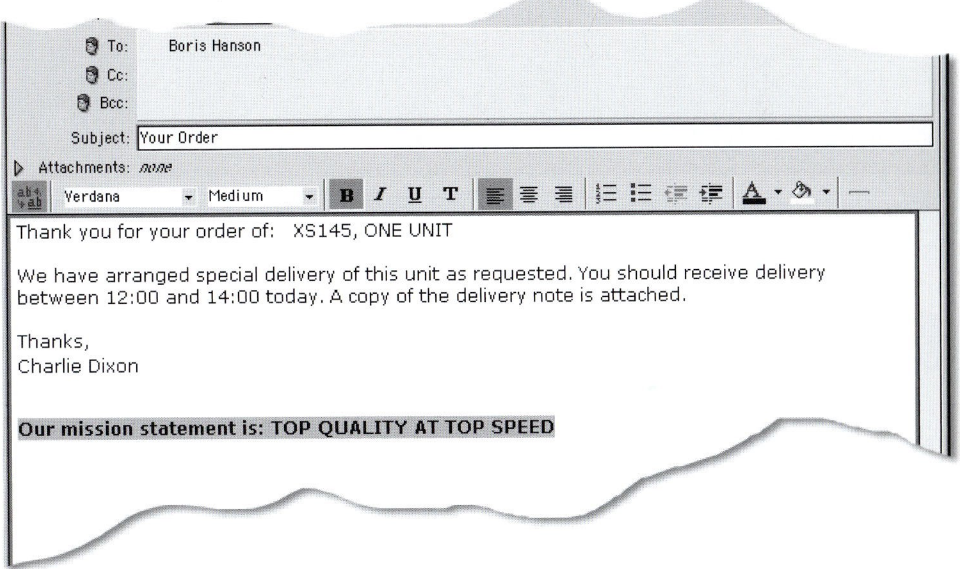
To: Boris Hanson
Cc:
Bcc:
Subject: Your Order
Attachments: none

Thank you for your order of: XS145, ONE UNIT

We have arranged special delivery of this unit as requested. You should receive delivery between 12:00 and 14:00 today. A copy of the delivery note is attached.

Thanks,
Charlie Dixon

Our mission statement is: TOP QUALITY AT TOP SPEED

Analysis
Whole group
5 minutes

What actions did you suggest to deal with this problem?
What actions did you promise?
Was your partner helpful and polite?
Did he / she use appropriate language for the telephone?

Self-assessment

Think about your performance on the tasks. Were you able to:

- explain and clarify a problem? ☐ yes ☐ need more practice
- predict consequences? ☐ yes ☐ need more practice
- suggest and promise action? ☐ yes ☐ need more practice

Unit 6 Make a recommendation

| Introduce a visual | Compare alternatives | Make a recommendation |

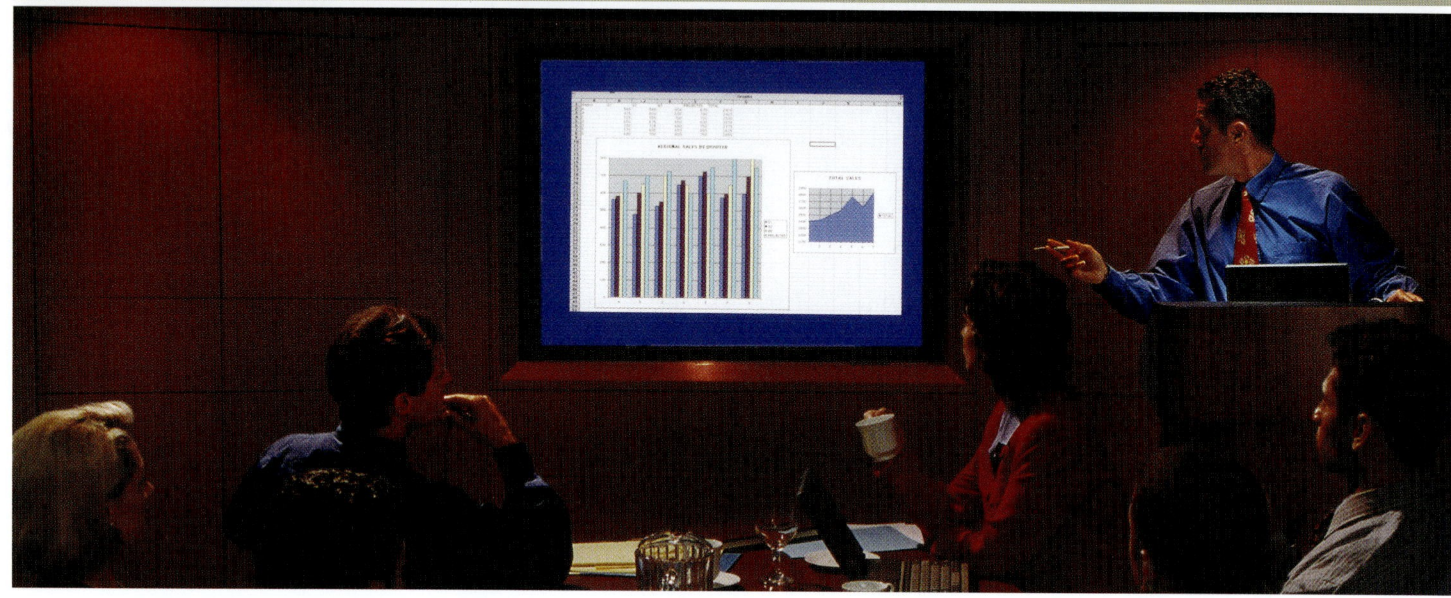

What do you think?
Whole group
10 minutes

Effective visual aids

Look at three visuals for a presentation about the photography industry and answer the questions.

1 Match each visual with the verbal message that goes with it.
  a Here you can see the rapid rise in sales of camera phones since 2001.
  b This chart shows that camera phones have the largest share of the market in 2004.
  c This table compares the sales of film cameras, digital cameras and camera phones from 2001 to 2005.

2 Discuss these questions.
  a Which visual do you think is the most attractive?
  b Which visual matches its purpose most effectively?
  c Which is the easiest to interpret?

1

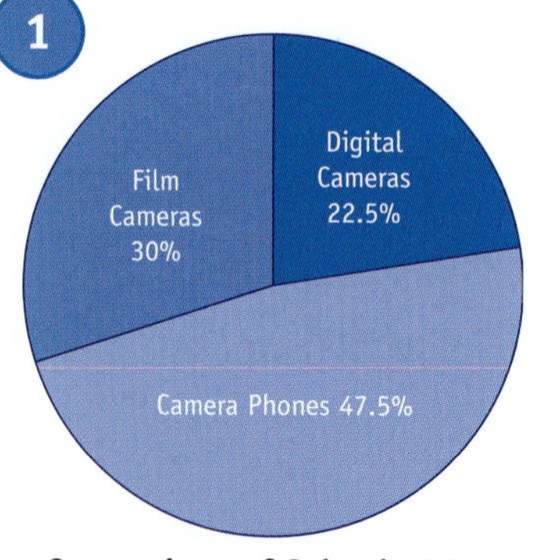

Comparison of Sales in 2004

2

Ringing the changes
Worldwide camera sales 2001-5 (units)

	Film cameras	Digital cameras	Camera phones
2001	68.7 m	12.5 m	6.2 m
2002	68.7 m	25 m	19 m
2003	62.5 m	31.2 m	31.2 m
2004	50 m	37.5 m	68.7 m
2005	37.5 m	43.7 m	131.2 m

3

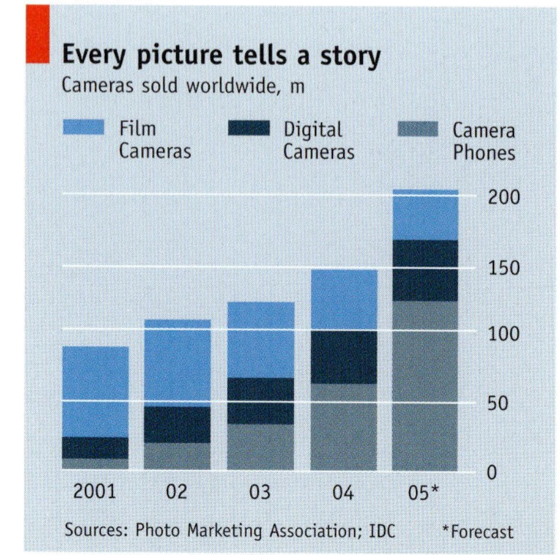

Good business practice, page 77

Task 1
Pairs
5 minutes

Objective: Introduce a visual

Look at charts A and B. Describe in one sentence what each chart shows. Compare your answers with the rest of the group.

A

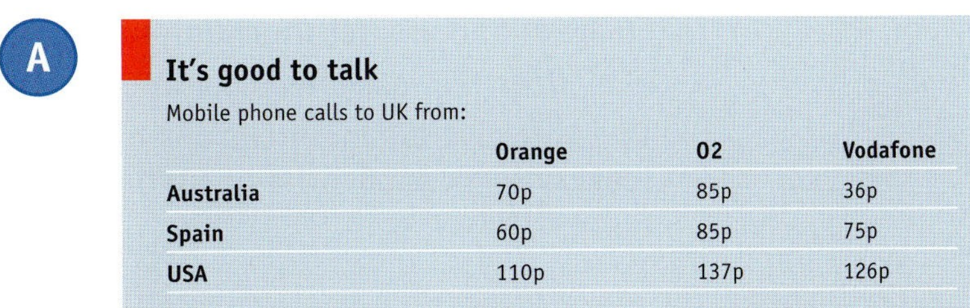

It's good to talk

Mobile phone calls to UK from:

	Orange	02	Vodafone
Australia	70p	85p	36p
Spain	60p	85p	75p
USA	110p	137p	126p

Prices as of June 2003

B

It's only words

Text messages to UK from:

	Orange	02	Vodafone
Australia	20p	30p	20p
Spain	30p	25p	37p
USA	35p	25p	35p

Prices as of June 2003

Task 2
Whole group
10 minutes

Objective: Compare alternatives

Allsop Trading, a UK company, has subsidiaries in Australia, Spain and the USA. Staff travel frequently between these countries and need to communicate with head office in the UK from their mobiles. Which of the three mobile phone service providers above should Allsop choose? Refer to the visuals and compare the alternatives.

Use the phrases below to direct the listener's attention to the visuals.

In chart A, you can see that ...

If you look at the column on the right, you will notice that ...

As you can see, ...

The important thing to notice here is that ...

Grammar reference: Comparatives and superlatives, page 92

CD 8 Listening
10 minutes

Listen to Lee Jones, the telecommunications manager at Allsop Trading and answer the questions.

1 Which of the three mobile phone service providers does he recommend in his short presentation to his colleagues? Does he reach the same conclusion as you?

2 Listen again and answer these questions.

  a How does Lee make his recommendation? What phrase does he use?

  b Does Lee give the main reasons for his choice ***before*** or ***after*** he makes his recommendation? Which order do you think is more effective?

What do you say?
Pairs
15 minutes

Comparing advantages

1 Look at the table, which compares three digital cameras. Then complete the sentences below.

Snapshot

A brief comparison of features of 3 digital cameras

	Pixel Tek 4000	Snap Happy	PhotoArt TF2
Price	€675	€420	€900
Weight	231 g	219 g	510 g
Image quality	****	***	*****
Time to download pictures to PC	****	*****	***
Ease of use	****	*****	***
Special features	none	Short video recording	Video and sound recording

Key: * worst / ***** best

The PhotoArt TF2 has several advantages:

One advantage is that ...

Another is that ...

However, there is a slight disadvantage in that ...

I would recommend the Snap Happy because ...

2 Look at the comparison of digital cameras again. Choose the one you would buy. Then present your choice to your partner. Give reasons by referring to the chart.

Culture at work

Factual or vague?

Some cultures use a lot of vague language, often understating or exaggerating the facts or leaving the true meaning unsaid. Other cultures believe that all statements should be strictly accurate and honest. How would you describe your culture? Complete your culture profile on page 82.

	Factual cultures	Vague cultures
Accuracy	Prefer to give precise details: e.g. The train was 13 minutes late; It's 26 minutes past 10.	Prefer to give approximate details: e.g. The train was a bit late; It's nearly 10:30.
Use of modifiers	Don't often use modifiers: e.g. The price is higher.	Often use modifiers: e.g. The price is a little higher.
Stating facts	State the facts exactly: e.g. We won't make the deadline.	Don't always state the facts exactly: e.g. We could have a slight problem meeting the deadline.

Look at these statements. Which are factual and which are vague?

- The rail service can be a bit slow sometimes.
- Four out of ten trains arrive more than 15 minutes late.
- The food is a little more expensive than you'd expect.
- The price of food is high – the average cost of one dish is €60.
- Two-thirds of customers said they were satisfied with the service.
- Most people seem to be quite pleased with the service.

Task 3

Objective: Make a recommendation

Individually
10 minutes

Step 1 Preparation

Think of three products to compare. Prepare a chart showing facts and figures for each product. Decide which one you would recommend.

Whole group
2–3 minutes
per presentation

Step 2 Presentation

Now present your chart and your recommendation to the rest of the group. Explain your reasons clearly.

Analysis
Whole group
5 minutes

Did the chart communicate the message effectively?
Were the reasons for the recommendation explained clearly?

Self-assessment

Think about your performance on the tasks. Were you able to:

- introduce a visual? ☐ yes ☐ need more practice
- compare alternatives? ☐ yes ☐ need more practice
- make a recommendation? ☐ yes ☐ need more practice

Writing 2 Memos

Write a short memo | Write a recommendation

What do you think?

1 A memo is an internal communication. Look quickly at the memo below. What do you notice about the layout?

2 Now read the memo and answer the questions.

1 Who sent it?
2 Who will read it?
3 What is the problem?
4 What is the background?
5 When will it be solved?

3 What do you think about the style of the memo? Is it more formal or informal?

Memo

To: All staff
From: The pay office
Subject: Delay in payment of salaries

We are sorry to inform you that there will be some delay in paying salaries this month. This is because of difficulties with the new computer system.

We will make every effort to solve the problem within the next two or three days and expect to be able to pay all salaries by the end of the month.

Thank you for your patience and understanding.

Task 1

Objective: Write a short memo

You work in the general administration office of a company. Write a memo to all staff to explain a future problem. Use these notes and follow the model above for your memo.

Grammar reference: Modal verbs, part 2, page 88

Notes

Problem:
Canteen closed during August

Background:
Renovation work

Promise:
Work to finish by end of August

Thanks

What do you write?

Following his presentation on mobile phone costs (see Unit 6), Lee Jones sent a memo making a recommendation. The sections of the memo a–g have been mixed up. Look at the framework below. Then order the sections of the memo appropriately by writing the letter for each section in the correct box.

a I have compared the cost of mobile phone calls from these countries using three different service providers: Orange, O2 and Vodafone.

My findings are as follows:

1) Vodafone compares well with the other providers on overall cost.

2) Vodafone is the cheapest for calls and text messages from Australia.

3) If we subscribe to Vodafone's international traveller service, we can obtain further discounts on calls from Spain and the USA. The cost of this service is £2.50 per phone per month.

b These findings show that Vodafone offers the best deal overall.

c You asked me to look at international mobile phone costs and make a recommendation.

d I recommend that we choose Vodafone as our service provider.

e The reason is that we need to reduce the cost of international mobile phone calls from Australia, Spain and the USA.

f To: Tom Barnes
From: Lee Jones
Subject: Recommendation for mobile phone provider

g I'm attaching the figures for you to study.

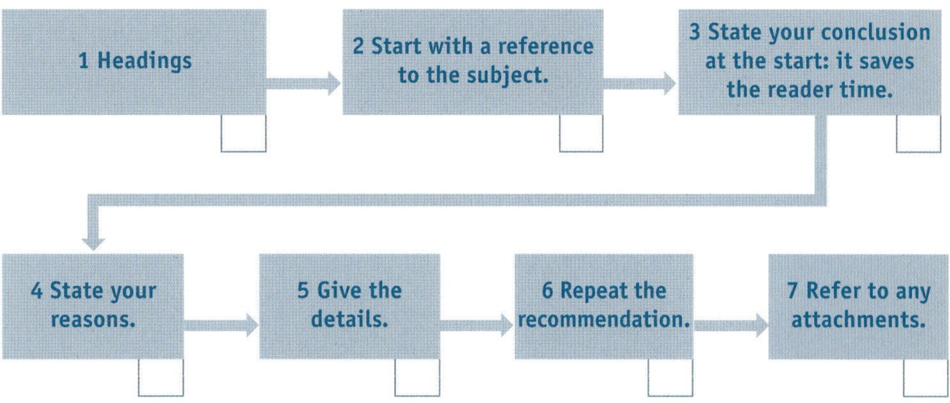

1 Headings
2 Start with a reference to the subject.
3 State your conclusion at the start: it saves the reader time.
4 State your reasons.
5 Give the details.
6 Repeat the recommendation.
7 Refer to any attachments.

Task 2

Objective: Write a recommendation

Using the chart that compares digital cameras in Unit 6, write a short memo recommending your choice of camera to a colleague who designs webpages.

OR

Choose a similar situation of your own and write a memo making a recommendation.

Unit 7 Brainstorm solutions

| Define the problem | Make suggestions and respond | Evaluate suggestions |

What do you think?
Pairs
10 minutes

Holding a brainstorming meeting

What is the best way to generate as many ideas as possible? Discuss the following points and tick the ones you both agree with. Change any others so that you can agree with them.

- ☐ A group of people is more creative than an individual working alone.
- ☐ People think more creatively in a relaxed atmosphere.
- ☐ It isn't necessary to have a leader at a brainstorming meeting.
- ☐ Everyone should feel that their opinions are valued.
- ☐ Criticism kills creativity.
- ☐ Discuss each idea as it comes up.
- ☐ Write all ideas on a board or flipchart.
- ☐ Don't bother to write down stupid ideas.
- ☐ Continue the session until there are no more ideas.

 Good business practice, page 78

Task 1
Pairs
15 minutes

Objective: Define the problem

Read the case study on page 35. Try to define the problem in two sentences:

The problem is ...
The company needs to ...

Whole group
5 minutes

Write all the definitions of the problem on the board. Choose the best one.

Case Study

Springfield is a chain of traditional department stores, selling a wide range of goods including clothing, electronic goods, kitchen items and china and glass. They have stores in all the major cities, occupying large and expensive buildings in city centre locations. But shoppers are deserting them. Sales have fallen by nearly 30 per cent, and they are losing market share to smaller, more specialised chains with a more modern image. The company hasn't made any profit for the past three years.

CD 9 Listening
Pairs
10 minutes

The senior managers of Springfield hold a brainstorming meeting to find a solution to the problem of falling sales. Listen to an extract from their meeting.

1 Do you think the leader performed his role effectively?
2 How did he respond to suggestions from the other managers? What did he say to each?

CD 10

Now listen to the second extract.

3 How did the leader ask for suggestions and ideas? What did he say?
4 How did the leader react when one participant criticised someone else's idea?
5 Do you think the leader's responses in the second extract were more effective in generating ideas? Why? /Why not?

What do you say?
10 minutes

Making suggestions

We make tentative suggestions when (a) we want to be very polite or (b) we are afraid that other people might not like our idea. Which of the following suggestions are tentative?

- ☐ How about if we change the displays more often.
- ☐ Why don't we hold some special events?
- ☐ What if we held some fashion shows?
- ☐ I think we should introduce more discount sales.
- ☐ I don't suppose we could invite some celebrities?
- ☐ Perhaps we could decorate in a more modern style.
- ☐ I suggest we move to smaller buildings.

Responding to suggestions

If you show your own opinion when responding to ideas – whether you are positive or negative – you may discourage further suggestions. Which of the responses below show the speaker's opinion and which are *neutral* (showing no opinion)? What else could you say?

- ☐ OK. Any other ideas?
- ☐ Yes – I like that!
- ☐ That's crazy – it would never work!
- ☐ Right – I've got that. What else?
- ☐ That's a good idea!
- ☐ That's interesting. Go on!

Task 2
Whole group
15 minutes

Objective: Make suggestions and respond

Now brainstorm the Springfield problem yourselves. Suggest anything you like – you may find that the pictures below give you some ideas. Choose someone to facilitate the meeting. The facilitator should write suggestions on the board and encourage people to contribute. Remember! It is important not to discuss or judge the ideas yet.

Analysis
5 minutes

Did the facilitator encourage you to contribute your ideas?
Did everyone in the group make a contribution? If not, why not?
Did you make tentative suggestions, or strong ones?
How did you react to other people's suggestions?

Culture at work

Decision-making

Cultures differ according to the ways in which they reach decisions. In some cultures, decisions are made by individuals with responsibility; in other cultures, decisions are reached by the consensus of everybody involved. How would you describe your culture? Complete your culture profile on page 82.

	Individualist cultures	Group cultures
Company organisation	Decisions are taken by senior managers.	Managers seek consensus from everyone involved.
Time	The decision-making process is short.	Decision-making takes a long time because everyone has to be consulted.
Implementation	It may take longer to implement decisions because of resistance to the idea.	Decisions, once taken, are stable and can be implemented without delay.
Problem-solving	Employees follow the lead of their managers.	Employees are encouraged to express opinions and come up with new ideas.

Task 3
Whole group
15 minutes

Objective: Evaluate suggestions

After collecting ideas, organise the suggestions you collected in Task 2 into three or four categories, e.g. cost saving, image, special customer attractions. Then evaluate the ideas and decide which *three* are the best. When evaluating each idea, ask the following questions.

Would this idea work?
How easily could we do it?
If we did this, what would happen?
Would we get the results we want?

Analysis
5 minutes

Were there a lot of workable ideas, or not many?
Did everyone in the group agree with the evaluations?
Was this an effective way to find a solution to the problem?

Grammar reference: Conditionals 1 and 2, page 89

Self-assessment

Think about your performance on the tasks. Were you able to:

- define the problem? ☐ yes ☐ need more practice
- make suggestions and respond? ☐ yes ☐ need more practice
- evaluate suggestions? ☐ yes ☐ need more practice

Unit 8 Get attention

| Open the presentation | Speak with emphasis | Refer to visuals |

What do you think?
Whole group
10 minutes

Getting the audience's attention

You have to make a presentation about finance, giving a lot of figures. How can you catch the attention of your audience? Tick all the strategies you would use.

- ☐ Skip the introduction to save time.
- ☐ Talk fast so that you finish sooner.
- ☐ Use simple language with short sentences.
- ☐ Give lots of details and background information.
- ☐ Show colourful visuals.
- ☐ Be enthusiastic.
- ☐ Speak calmly and quietly – this is a serious subject.
- ☐ Read from a carefully prepared script.
- ☐ Keep eye contact with the audience.
- ☐ Ask questions from time to time.

Now share your opinions with the rest of the group.

Good business practice, page 76

CD 11 Listening 1
Pairs
5 minutes

1 **If you want your audience to listen to you, you need strategies to make the opening sentences of your presentation interesting. Listen to the examples a–c and match them with the strategies 1–3.**

Examples

a ___________

b ___________

c ___________

Strategies

1 Ask the audience a question.
2 Give an interesting fact or statistic.
3 Show why your presentation is especially interesting or relevant for your audience.

2 **Discuss what presenters usually do in your company / country. Which strategy would you prefer to use?**

Task 1
Pairs
10 minutes preparation
1 minute to present each idea

Objective: Open the presentation

Choose one of the situations below and decide on an interesting way to open the presentation. Be ready to demonstrate your idea.

Situation 1

You have to explain to your team how you plan to cut costs by 15% next year without losing any jobs.

Situation 2

Tell your colleagues in the sales department how sales increased after reducing the price of a product.

Situation 3

You are a factory manager. Report to the directors that productivity has increased by 8% since investing €2 million in new machinery last year.

Analysis
5 minutes

Which strategy did each pair choose?
Did their opening make you want to listen to the whole presentation?

Culture at work

Formal and informal presentations

In some cultures, people expect business presentations to be formal. They don't believe that an informal presentation can be serious. Other cultures prefer presentations to be informal and think that formal presentations are dull and ineffective. How would you describe your culture? Complete your culture profile on page 82.

	Formal	Informal
Dress	Business suit, e.g. jacket and tie for a man	Casual
Body language	Tightly controlled; limited	A lot of movement and gestures
Relationship to audience	Not much interaction with the audience; no use of humour	A lot of interaction – asking and answering questions; use of humour
Language	Professional or technical vocabulary; longer sentences; more elaborate expressions	Everyday expressions and even slang

What do you say?

Giving numbers

Since large numbers are difficult to understand, you can help your audience by writing them down. When describing large amounts, round the figures up or down (as appropriate) or give an approximate number.

1 Match the numbers a–h with the expressions for approximate or rounded numbers 1–8.

a	495,802	1	only about twenty thousand
b	69 per cent	2	just over a thousand
c	1041	3	more than six hundred dollars
d	21,560	4	nearly half a million
e	267,000	5	nearly everybody
f	98.4 per cent of people	6	approximately a quarter of a million
g	$604	7	just under eighty billion
h	79,766,922,603	8	roughly two thirds

2 Which expression(s) indicate an amount is relatively small?

3 Which one(s) indicate you think an amount is too much?

Grammar reference: The language of change, page 93.

CD 12 Listening 2
10 minutes

Listen to an extract from a presentation comparing sales of PDAs (Personal Digital Assistants, or handheld computers) with Smartphones (phones that connect to the internet).

1 As you listen, underline the words that are most stressed in the script below.

2 Mark the places where the speaker pauses (||). The first sentence has been marked as an example.

The handheld computer is dead, || and the future is in Smartphones. || How do I know? Just look at the figures. As you can see, sales of PDAs have stayed flat at around eleven million units worldwide. What about sales of Smartphones? They're rising fast from just four million last year to nearly twelve million this year. The PDA market will never be a mass market. Almost everyone who wants a PDA now has one.

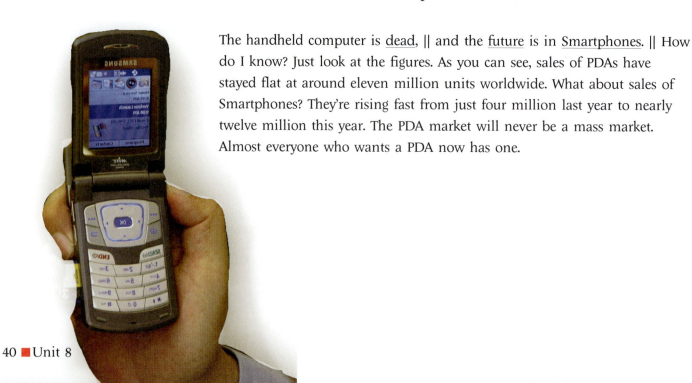

Task 2
15-20 minutes

Objective: Speak with emphasis

Step 1 Rehearse

Practise reading the extract about PDAs and Smartphones. Try to sound like the presenter.

Step 2 Speak with emphasis

Mark the script below in the same way as in Listening 2. Then practise reading the script with as much emphasis as you can. Stress key words. Add pauses for effect.

Technology spending by US companies goes in long-term cycles. If you look at the graph, it's clear that big leaps in new technology happen roughly every 15 years. This leads to a spending boom, followed by relative calm. Right now spending is increasing – but only by two per cent. In the late 1990s, growth was 11 per cent. While back in the early 80s, it was as high as 16 per cent.

Analysis
5 minutes

Did you read slowly and clearly?
Did you stress the key words?
Did you pause in the right places?
Did you sound enthusiastic?

Task 3
Individually
10 minutes

Objective: Refer to visuals

Step 1 Preparation

Choose one of the graphs on page 103 and prepare a short description of it. You may want to use the following phrases.

fell sharply/ slightly	*rose steadily*	*fluctuated mildly*
a sudden increase	*a dramatic fall*	*reached a high/ a low*

Next prepare an interesting way to introduce your graph.

Groups of 3-4
2 minutes
per presentation

Step 2 Presentation

Refer to the graph and explain what it shows to the others in your group. Remember to speak with emphasis. You may want to use the following phrases.

As you can see ... *You'll notice that ...*
This part of the graph clearly shows ...

Analysis
5 minutes

Did the presenter find an interesting way to introduce the topic?
Was it easy to follow the meaning?
Did they speak clearly and enthusiastically?

Self-assessment

Think about your performance on the tasks. Were you able to:

– open the presentation?	☐ yes	☐ need more practice
– speak with emphasis?	☐ yes	☐ need more practice
– refer to visuals?	☐ yes	☐ need more practice

Unit 9 Make small talk

| Introduce topics | Keep it moving | End politely |

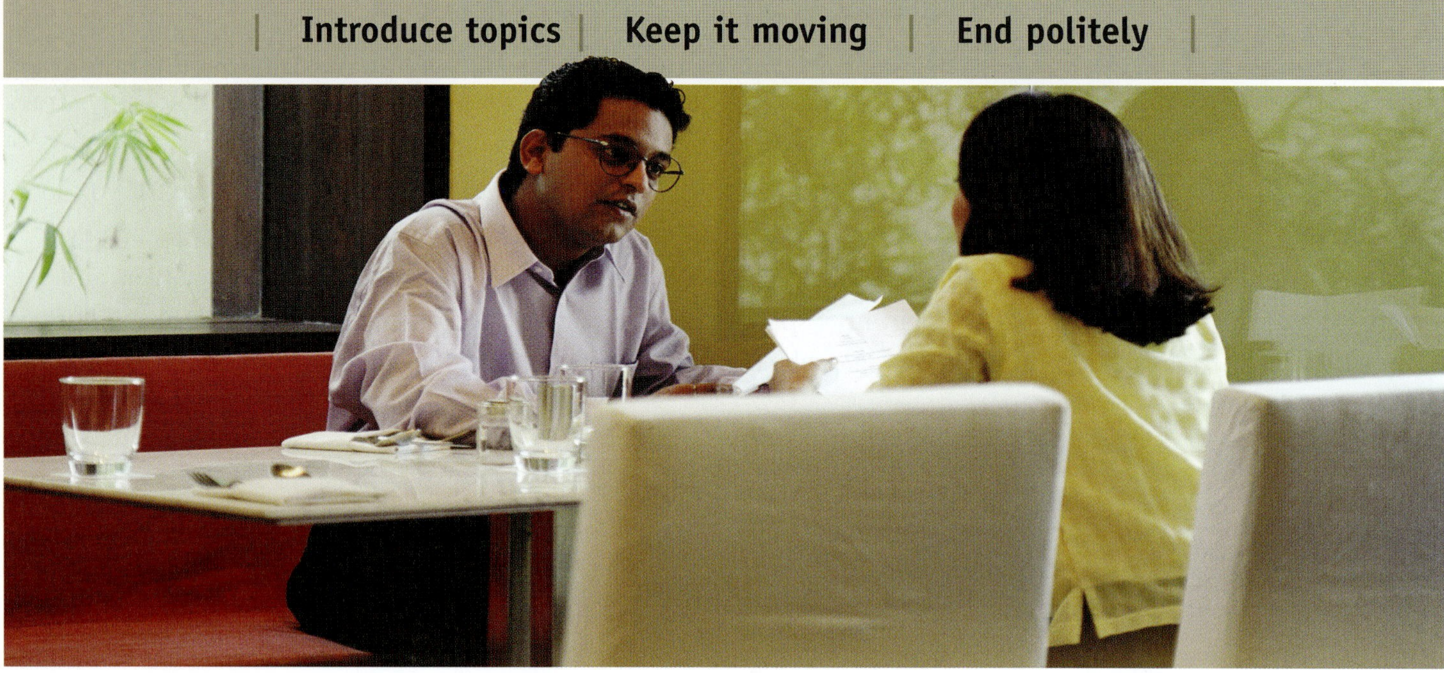

What do you think?
Whole group
10 minutes

Topics for small talk

Many people say that the worst part of a business meeting is lunch! When you don't know your business partner very well, it can be difficult to find 'safe' non-business topics.

1 Look at the topics below and discuss which ones are safe and which might cause offence. If there are different nationalities in your group, find out if they have different opinions.

Personal topics:

Family
Marriage or relationships
Hobbies or special interests
Religious beliefs

General interest topics:

Films
Sport
Travel
Art and architecture

The other person's country:

Climate
Political situation
Food / Customs
History

Topics people have strong opinions about:

World affairs
Social problems
Environment
Money

2 Can you think of other examples of safe topics or topics that might cause offence?

Good business practice, page 81

CD 13, 14 Listening
20 minutes

1 Listen to two conversations. What topics do the people talk about?

1 Gerry and Serena have lunch together as part of a business meeting.
2 Milo and Paul say goodbye at the end of a meeting.

CD 13

2 Listen to the first conversation again and answer the questions.

a How does Serena introduce the topic of the restaurant? Does she ask a question, make a comment or give some new information?
b How does Serena respond to Gerry's statements ...
'This building used to be a railway station.'
'It has a very good atmosphere.'
c Gerry tries to continue the subject of jazz. Does he ask a question, make a comment or give some new information?
d Serena says she doesn't know much about jazz. Then she throws the question back to Gerry. What does she say here?

CD 14

3 Listen to the second conversation again and answer the questions.

a How does Milo bring up the subject of travelling home?
b How does Paul respond when Milo says that the traffic is not so bad after six?
c How does Paul respond when Milo tells him, 'It could take you an hour to get to the airport.'
d How did Milo end the conversation with Paul? Was he polite? What was his excuse for leaving?

What do you say?
5 minutes

Useful responses

Choose the best response to each piece of news. (More than one answer may be possible in some cases.)

1 Coming back from New York, our plane was delayed by ten hours!
2 They've closed that nice restaurant we went to last time.
3 Did you know that we have two cathedrals in this city?
4 We have a new baby in the family – a little boy!
5 Our local football team has qualified for the European Cup!
6 In my country, men love to go shopping.

a That's interesting!
b Congratulations!
c That's too bad!
d How terrible!
e That's amazing!
f Fantastic!

Practice
Small groups
5 minutes

Each person should prepare some examples of good news, bad news and surprising news. Give your 'news' to others in your group. Practise responding appropriately.

What do you say?
5 minutes

Endings

Read some ideas for ending a conversation 1–3. Match them with the situations a–c.

1 Well, it's been nice talking to you.
2 Oh dear, look at the time! We'd better get back to work.
3 I'm afraid I've got to rush – I've got a train to catch!

a The end of the day
b A conversation with someone at a party
c A conversation by the coffee machine in the office

Task 1
Pairs
10 minutes

Objective: Introduce topics

Have a conversation with your partner. Try to introduce each of your topics in a natural way.

Partner A turn to page 99. Choose two topics.
Partner B turn to page 102. Choose two topics.

Analysis
5 minutes

What topics did your partner introduce?
How did he / she introduce them?
Did your conversation feel comfortable and natural?

Task 2
Pairs
10 minutes

Objective: Keep it moving

Choose a topic you and your partner would both like to talk about. One of you should introduce the topic. Try to keep the conversation going for as long as you can. If you can't continue the same topic, introduce a new one.

Analysis
5 minutes

Did you manage to talk continuously, or were there some silent moments?
Did your partner respond to what you said? How?
Did your partner use the 'throw it back' technique?

Grammar reference: Questions, page 86

Culture at work

Attitudes to personal space

Each of us has a concept of personal space and we don't like it when someone we don't know intrudes into our privacy. The extent and size of our personal or private space varies by culture. People with large personal space prefer to keep their distance from others.

How would you describe your culture? Do people have small or large personal space? Complete your culture profile on page 82.

	People with small personal space ...	People with large personal space ...
How close?	stand close together when talking.	feel uncomfortable when standing too close to others.
Touching	often touch each other as a sign of friendliness.	may shake hands, but don't generally touch the people they work with.
Familiarity with strangers	are easy to get to know.	are reserved with people they don't know well.
Personal topics	are happy to discuss personal matters with people they don't know well.	don't discuss personal matters in a business relationship.
The home as private space	are more likely to invite you to their home.	are unlikely to invite you to their home.

Task 3
Groups of 3-4
15 minutes

Objective: End politely

Role-play these situations with your partners. Take about five minutes for each situation. You should only discuss general topics.

Situation 1

It's 9:00. You are waiting for a meeting which can't start until the chairperson arrives. Make conversation until she comes.

Situation 2

You are in a restaurant having lunch together. You have ordered the food. Make conversation while you wait for it to be served.

Situation 3

It's the end of the day after a long meeting together. You are all a bit tired. Make conversation for a few minutes before making an excuse to leave.

Analysis
5 minutes

How did your conversations go?
Did you talk fluently and naturally?
How did you end each one?

Self-assessment

Think about your performance on the tasks. Were you able to:

- introduce topics? ☐ yes ☐ need more practice
- keep it moving? ☐ yes ☐ need more practice
- end politely? ☐ yes ☐ need more practice

Writing 3 Short factual reports

| Report trends | Comment on the figures |

What do you think?

1 Which is better in a short factual report?

a ☐ a single long paragraph or ☐ points organised under headings?
b ☐ long complicated sentences or ☐ short simple sentences?
c ☐ as many details as possible or ☐ focus on key points only?

2 The table shows the sales figures for three products during the first quarter. Actual sales are compared with the target for each month, and for the quarter as a whole.

Complete the paragraph below with the following phrases.

were above target *an increase*
were just below target *increased steadily*

On Target

Q1 actual sales vs forecast for products X5-X7

Product	X5		X6		X7	
	Target	Actual	Target	Actual	Target	Actual
January	500	491	450	448	300	320
February	500	512	450	435	300	295
March	500	523	450	469	300	281
Totals	**1500**	**1526**	**1350**	**1352**	**900**	**896**

Product X5

Sales of X5 [1] ________ through the first quarter. Sales [2] ________ in January, but [3] ________ in February and March, and for the quarter as a whole. We forecast [4] ________ in sales to around 1550 during the second quarter.

Task 1

Objective: Report trends

Write similar short paragraphs for Products X6 and X7. Point out that sales of X7 will probably decrease because it is an old model and newer models are coming on the market in the spring.

Grammar reference: Linking sentences and ideas: relative clauses, page 95

What do you write? **The graph shows the number of tourists arriving at the main airport of a Mediterranean island. A report on the figures for the year follows. Complete the report below with words and phrases from the box.**

a disappointing month   failed to reach   only   over   poor
an improvement   significant   the normal pattern   ~~promising~~   well

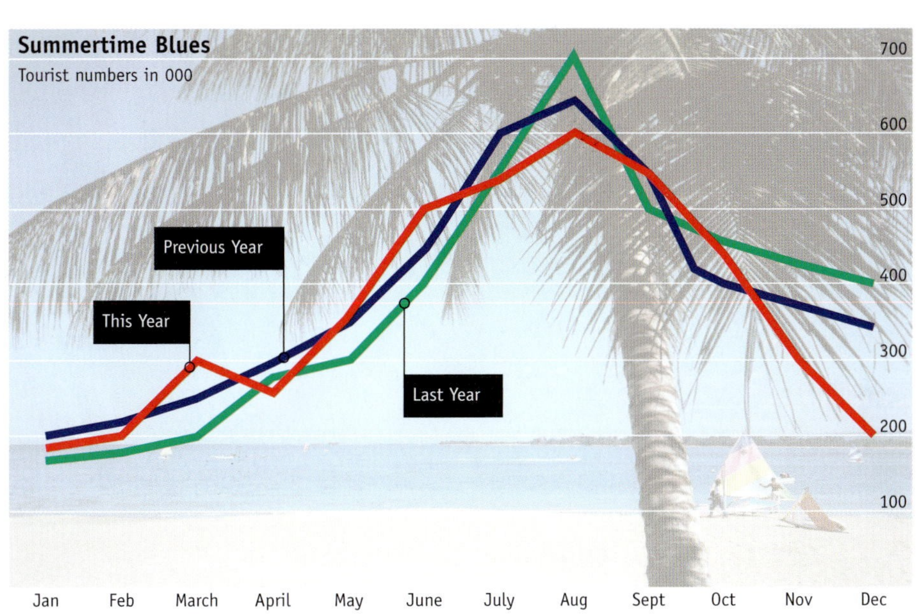

Not so high season

Despite a promising start tourist numbers failed to hit the highs of last year

First quarter We saw a [1] promising start to the year, with tourist numbers increasing steadily to around 300,000 in March. This compares [2] ____________ with the figure of 200,000 for March last year.

Second quarter April was [3] ____________ with only 250,000 tourists arriving. But this was followed by an increase in the numbers in June, reaching a total of [4] ____________ half a million. Most of the visitors who travel in June are single people and couples, so this high figure is [5] ____________.

Third quarter Tourist numbers [6] ____________ the usual peak levels in August. The total number reached [7] ____________ 600,000 compared to 700,000 last year. However, the figure fell only slightly to 550,000 in September, which was [8] ____________ on last year.

Fourth quarter Tourist numbers dropped towards the end of the year, which is [9] ____________. However, the number of tourist arrivals in December was nearly 50 per cent lower than last year. This is a [10] ____________ result for the Christmas period.

Task 2 **Objective: Comment on the figures**

Write a similar report on tourist numbers during the previous year. Refer to the blue line on the graph above.

Unit 10 Present an argument

| Give reasons | Stress key words | Present a structured argument |

Task 1
Whole group
10 minutes

Objective: Give reasons

Why do companies need to invest in the following kinds of software?

- Anti-virus software
- Firewalls
- Spam filters

Try to use the following language for giving your reasons.
because / because of *due to* *in order to* *so that* *the reason is*

What do you think?
Pairs
10 minutes

Making a strong case

Two IT managers argue for an increase in the budget for internet security. Read their arguments. Which makes the case more strongly? Why?

Fergus Mathews

'Well, as you know, using the internet is becoming more dangerous all the time. Attacks from viruses are becoming more frequent and they are affecting more and more people. And there's also the risk of fraud: hackers stealing the customers' bank details and so on. I don't want to have to economise on expenditure for developing more secure systems. Remember what happened last year? Hackers were able to access our customer database and some highly confidential information was stolen. If I'd had a bigger budget last year, I'd have been able to protect that data more effectively. I need an increase in my budget. I can't make the system secure on the budget I've got.'

Dervla O'Connor

'I'd like to propose an increase in the budget of 15 per cent. That may seem a lot, but there are two very good reasons why we need this increase.

'Firstly because online sales are increasingly important to us. More than 55 per cent of our customers buy via the internet, and this figure is growing every year. But people won't buy online if they are worried about the risks. So we must make sure that our systems are trustworthy.

'Secondly because of internet crime. Internet criminals are becoming more and more sophisticated. So we need to increase our efforts in order to stay ahead. That means increasing what we spend on up-dating and improving our systems.

'The internet offers enormous benefits to us. If we want to make the most of this potential, we must develop the best possible security systems. That's why I'm proposing a substantial increase in the security budget.'

Now report your conclusions to the rest of the group.

Good business practice, page 77

What do you say?
5 minutes

Structuring the argument

In Dervla O'Connor's argument (above), what phrases are used for the following?

1 to introduce a series of reasons? ________________

2 to introduce different reasons in a sequence? ________________

3 to repeat the main proposal in the conclusion? ________________

Read phrases a–f below. Match them with their function 1, 2 or 3 above.

a One reason is ...

b I'd like to explain the reasons for this.

c It is therefore very important to ...

d The second reason is ...

e There are a number of reasons why we need to take action.

f What's more ...

Grammar reference: Linking sentences and ideas, page 95

CD 15 Listening
5 minutes

A sports shoe manufacturer has a problem. A pirate company is making counterfeit shoes, which are of inferior quality. The production director proposes a system of electronic ID tags which will make the company's own products easy to identify.

1 Structuring the argument

Listen to the speaker's argument and answer the questions.

1 In what order does he present the following reasons for his proposal?
   a to be able to offer guarantees
   b to maximise return on investment
   c to reassure the customers

2 How does the speaker begin the argument?
   a He asks a question.
   b He specifies the topic.
   c He describes a problem.

3 What sentence does he use to introduce the reasons for his proposal?

4 What is his concluding sentence?

2 Stressing key words

Listen again and notice the way the presenter speaks.

1 Does he present the argument *strongly* or *neutrally*?

2 Which words does he stress? Write down as many key words as you can. Then compare your list with the rest of the group.

Task 2
Pairs
10 minutes

Objective: Stress key words

Look at Dervla O'Connor's argument on page 49. Which words do you think should be stressed? Then look at page 99. The words in bold are the words that should be most stressed when speaking. Practise reading the argument aloud. Stress the words in bold.

Culture at work

Showing feelings

In some cultures, people are not afraid to show their feelings when arguing for an idea or a proposal they really believe in. In other cultures, people prefer to stay cool. How would you describe your culture? Complete your culture profile on page 82.

	People who show feelings ...	People who stay cool ...
Language	make use of strong and exaggerated language.	use neutral language without exaggeration.
Gestures and body language	use big gestures and facial expressions.	speak in a calm and controlled manner.
Showing reactions	may respond emotionally to other people's arguments.	don't show what they're thinking when they listen to other people's arguments.

Task 3
Individually

Objective: Present a structured argument

In M. Power & Co Ltd, any employee can put forward a proposal 'for the benefit of the company and its staff'. People with the best ideas are invited to present their proposals at a special meeting.

15 minutes

Step 1 Preparation

Choose one of the proposals below, or think of your own idea. Organise your reasons into a logical order. Be ready to explain and emphasise each reason. Then prepare a short introduction and conclusion. You can follow the model from the Listening activity.

Proposal 1

To install security cameras around the company's premises
Reasons:
- Need to prevent industrial espionage
- Cameras are effective in detecting any unauthorised persons
- Company has a lot of confidential research data

Proposal 2

To build a gym for the staff on company premises
Reasons:
- Increase staff motivation
- Reduce stress in the workplace
- Encourage staff to stay fit

Proposal 3

To produce umbrellas with the company logo and have them available in reception
Reasons:
- Promote the company name
- Impress company guests
- Help staff on rainy days

2–3 minutes

Step 2 Presentation

Present your argument to the rest of the group.

Analysis
5 minutes

How did each presenter organise their argument?
Was the argument logical and effective?
Did the presenter make an effective conclusion?

Self-assessment

Think about your performance on the tasks. Were you able to:

- give reasons? ☐ yes ☐ need more practice
- stress key words? ☐ yes ☐ need more practice
- present a structured argument? ☐ yes ☐ need more practice

Unit 11 Negotiate

| Make proposals | Respond to proposals | Negotiate a win–win solution |

Task 1
Pairs
5 minutes

Objective: Make proposals

A rich friend is offering to give you and your partner $100 if you can agree how to split it. You are not allowed to split it 50:50. You can't say 70:30 or 60:40 and make a side deal to adjust the amounts later. You have *one minute* to think about what you want and *one minute* to negotiate a deal with your partner.

Try to use the following language in your discussion.

Make proposals

Let's ...
Why don't we ... ?
I suggest we ...
I think we should ...
How about ... ?

Respond

That's fine with me.
OK – it's a deal!
Maybe another option would be ...
I think it might be better to ...
I'm sorry – I can't agree to that.
No way!

Analysis
5 minutes

Did you and your partner reach agreement? If so, how?
Did you try to win more than your partner?
Did you try to find a way in which you could both feel happy?

Possible solutions, page 104

What do you think?
Pairs
10 minutes

Negotiation strategies

1 **What is the best approach to negotiation? The *win–win* approach, where both you and the other person can feel happy with the outcome, or the *I win–you lose* approach, where the strongest person gets the bigger share?**

2 **Which of these strategies are best for finding a win–win solution in a negotiation?**

- ☐ If you don't agree, say 'no'.
- ☐ Support your proposals with reasons and arguments.
- ☐ Ask questions to find out what your partner's position is.
- ☐ Keep repeating your demands.
- ☐ Look for alternative solutions.
- ☐ Take time to think.

Good business practice, page 81

CD 16 Listening
10 minutes

Viktor, a supplier, talks to two of his buyers, Xavier and Yacoub, about new delivery charges. Listen to the two negotiations and answer the questions.

1 Which buyer is more likely to reach an agreement with Viktor?
2 How does Xavier respond in the first negotiation?
3 How does Yacoub respond in the second negotiation?
4 In the second negotiation, how does Viktor respond to the proposal?

Culture at work

The importance of relationships

There are big differences in the way that people from different cultures conduct negotiations. In some cultures, business partners form long-term relationships . In other cultures, the relationship lasts only as long as the contract. How would you describe your culture? Complete your culture profile on page 82.

	Long-term relationships	Short-term relationships
Small talk	Small talk is important for getting to know people on a personal level before starting to discuss business.	Work is separated from private life. When discussing business, it is considered a waste of time to talk about personal matters.
Time	People are willing to invest a lot of personal time in relationships. Socialising outside office hours is essential.	Apart from lunch breaks, not much time is given to socialising.
The basis for reaching agreement	You won't reach an agreement unless you like and trust your business partners.	People reach agreement on the basis of strong arguments; e.g. this is the best product / price.

What do you say?
5 minutes

Responding to proposals

1 What do you say in a negotiation when the other person makes an offer you don't want to accept?

2 The following language is from the Listening. Match each sentence 1–10 with a strategy a–h.

1 There's no way! None of your competitors charge for deliveries.
2 I see. Well, I can understand your position.
3 How much are you thinking of charging?
4 Do you mean five per cent of the order value on each delivery?
5 Let me think …
6 Here's another idea. How about a flat rate of – say …
7 You'd gain because you wouldn't have to deliver so often.
8 So you're saying you'd be willing to buy in larger quantities?
9 I'll need to do some calculations to see how that would work.
10 It sounds like a reasonable idea, but …

Strategies

☐ a Say that you agree in principle
☐ b Dismiss the offer completely
☐ c Make a neutral response
☐ d Give yourself time to think (two answers)
☐ e Make an alternative proposal
☐ f Stress the benefits of your idea to the other person
☐ g Clarify (two answers)
☐ h Ask for more information

Grammar reference: Gerunds and infinitives, page 96

Task 2
Pairs
5 minutes

Objective: Respond to proposals

Step 1 Preparation

How many different solutions can you find to each situation below? Choose a role and prepare several proposals.

5 minutes

Step 2 Response

Act out the conversation. Respond to your partner's proposals using the language from 'What do you say?'

Situation 1

Role A: Team leader

Your team has to complete a contract by Wednesday next week. The only way to complete it on time is for the whole team to work over the weekend. You don't think it would be fair on the group if one team member was excused.

Role B: Team member

It's your young son's birthday on Saturday.

You have organised a party for friends and relatives starting at 3 pm.

5 minutes

Situation 2

Hardgraft Inc. is merging with Freetime plc. Hardgraft employees have 20 days' holiday per year while Freetime employees have 35 days per year. How can you reach a compromise on holidays?

Role A (Hardgraft Inc.)

You think more than 25 days' holiday would be too much. It's better to reward people with high pay, linked to performance and length of time with the company.

Role B (Freetime plc)

You think that reducing staff holiday entitlement would greatly upset your staff and result in poor motivation. Maybe 30 days a year would be acceptable to employees if other benefits were offered.

Analysis
5 minutes

How many solutions did you find for the two situations?
Did your partner respond in a helpful way to your proposals?

Task 3

Pairs
10 minutes

Objective: Negotiate a win-win solution

Step 1 Preparation

The sales manager of Butternut Co. has booked a conference room in the Admiral Hotel for a meeting with regional sales agents (30 people). The booking is for Wednesday next week. The bookings manager at the hotel phones the sales manager about the booking.

15 minutes

Step 2 Negotiate an agreement

Role A (Bookings Manager) turn to page 99.
Role B (Sales Manager) turn to page 102.

Analysis
5 minutes

Describe to the rest of the group what happened in your negotiation.
Did you find a win-win solution?
Was your partner flexible and creative in making alternative proposals?

Self-assessment

Think about your performance on the tasks. Were you able to:

– make proposals?	☐ yes	☐ need more practice
– respond to proposals?	☐ yes	☐ need more practice
– negotiate a win-win solution?	☐ yes	☐ need more practice

Unit 12 Participate in meetings

| Put your point of view | Listen and take turns | Make your case and respond |

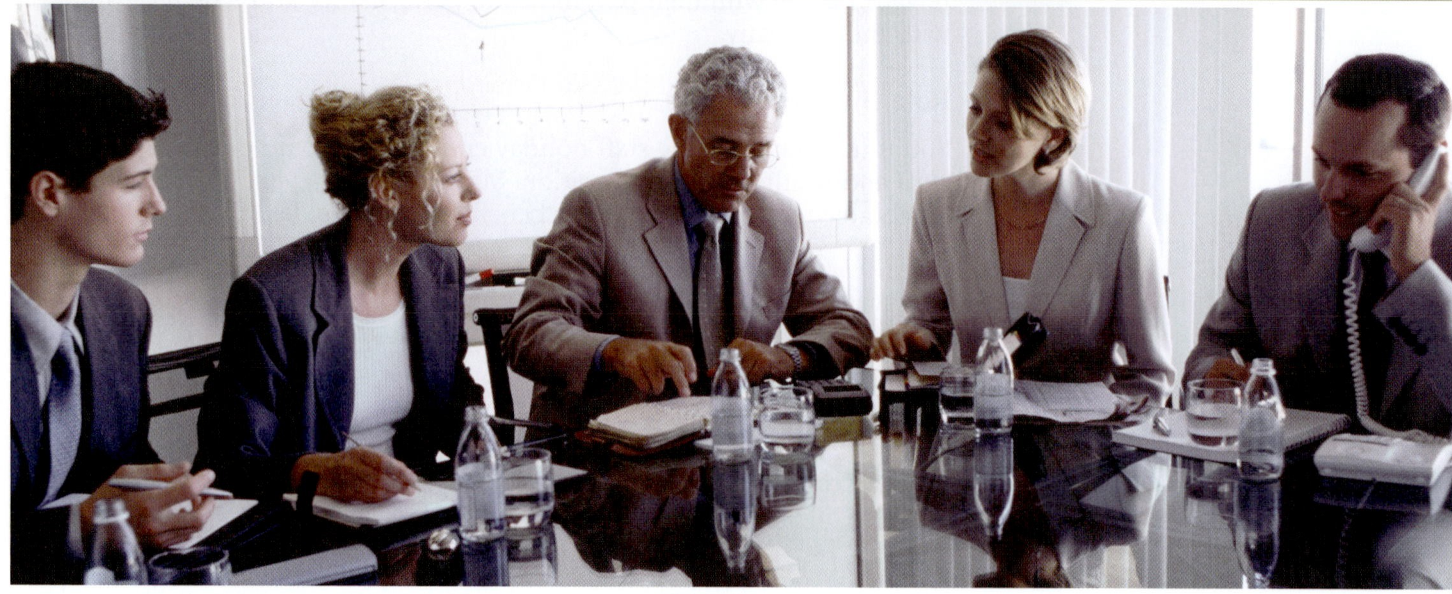

Task 1
Groups of up to 6
5 minutes

Objective: Put your point of view

'Most meetings are a waste of time.' What do you think about this viewpoint? Put your own viewpoint to the others in the group.

You may want to use some of the following language.

I agree that ...	*I'm not sure ...*
Don't you think ... ?	*Wouldn't you agree that ... ?*
It's obvious that ...	*We all know that ...*

Analysis
5 minutes

Did everyone in the group manage to put their viewpoint across?
Did everyone listen to the others' viewpoints?
What were the opinions of others in your group?
If someone wasn't able to contribute their idea, why was that?

What do you think?
Pairs
10 minutes

Making meetings more effective

When you attend a meeting, what should you do to achieve your own objectives and help make the meeting more effective? Look at the list on page 57. Tick the points you both agree with. Then compare your ideas with the rest of the group.

Before the meeting

- ☐ Read the minutes of the previous meeting (and other relevant documents).
- ☐ Make up your mind about key issues and be prepared to convince everyone that you are right.

During the meeting

- ☐ Make only relevant and interesting points.
- ☐ Make sure everyone understands your point of view.
- ☐ Speak loudly and repeat your ideas often.
- ☐ Listen carefully to other people's points of view.
- ☐ Don't say anything because you might sound stupid.
- ☐ Don't discuss too much because you want to finish the meeting quickly.
- ☐ Avoid any conflicts or disagreements.
- ☐ Find out what different people think.
- ☐ Try to reach a conclusion that everyone can feel satisfied with.

Good business practice, page 78

What do you say?
5 minutes

Responding and turn-taking

In a meeting, it is important to be able to respond appropriately to what others are saying and to get your turn to speak. Match each phrase a–f with its function 1–6.

Function

1. Agree and add another argument in support
2. Put an alternative point of view
3. Correct a mistake or misunderstanding
4. Get your turn to speak.
5. Deal with an interruption
6. Bring up a new point or argument

Phrase

- a Can I come in here?
- b I have a point to raise about ...
- c Sorry, but that's not quite right.
- d That's right! And I'd also like to point out that ...
- e But don't you think ... ?
- f Can I just finish?

What other phrases can you add for each function?

CD 17 Listening
10 minutes

1 **Arctic Foods is a company that produces frozen packaged food such as beefburgers. A group of managers discuss a proposal to change the recipe of a popular product so that it contains less fat. Listen to six short extracts from the meeting and match each extract with a function below.**

a Agree and add another argument in support ☐
b Put an alternative point of view ☐
c Correct a mistake or misunderstanding ☐
d Get your turn to speak ☐
e Deal with an interruption ☐
f Bring up a new point or argument ☐

2 **What phrase do the speakers use for each function?**

Task 2
Groups of 3-4
5-10 minutes per topic

Objective: Listen and take turns

Choose a topic and follow the framework below. Each person should give their viewpoint and speak for about one minute. Then continue discussing the topic, or change roles and repeat the four steps with a different topic.

Topics

1 We should boycott tourism to countries which have oppressive regimes.
2 We should ban TV advertising which is aimed specifically at children.
3 If we want to reduce traffic, we should make people pay to drive in the city centre.
4 It isn't right to claim against a food company because its products are fattening.
5 It is better to buy local products than products imported from other countries.

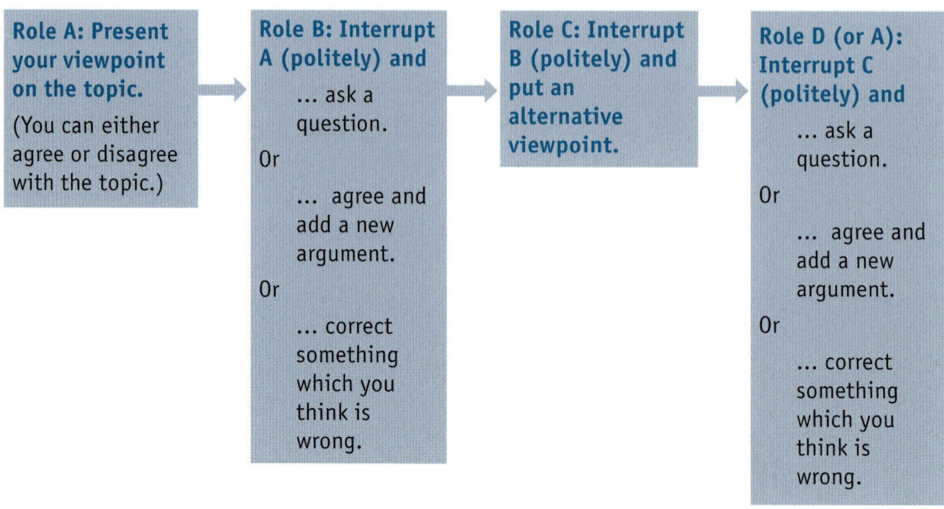

Role A: Present your viewpoint on the topic.
(You can either agree or disagree with the topic.)
Role B: Interrupt A (politely) and
... ask a question.
Or
... agree and add a new argument.
Or
... correct something which you think is wrong.
Role C: Interrupt B (politely) and put an alternative viewpoint.
Role D (or A): Interrupt C (politely) and
... ask a question.
Or
... agree and add a new argument.
Or
... correct something which you think is wrong.

Analysis
5 minutes

How well did each person listen?
Did everyone get an equal turn at speaking?
Did everyone interrupt politely?

Grammar reference: Modal verbs, part 2, page 88

Culture at work

Attitudes to silence during discussions

We can distinguish between three styles of communication: Anglo-Saxon, Latin and Asian. How would you describe your culture? Complete your culture profile on page 82.

> **Anglo-Saxon:** People feel uncomfortable when there is silence. When one person stops speaking, another starts. It isn't polite to interrupt.
>
> **Latin:** People are very talkative and feel uncomfortable when there is silence. People frequently interrupt each other. This is not impolite but shows interest in what the other person is saying.
>
> **Asian:** There is often a silence between the moment when one person stops speaking and the next person begins. It is a sign of respect for the other person if you take time to think silently about what they said.

Task 3
Groups of 4
25 minutes

Objective: Make your case and respond

Read the situation, look at your role brief and discuss the proposal. Make your case according to your brief, but remember to listen to what others are saying. Think about how to get your turn to speak and how to respond appropriately. It doesn't matter if you don't reach agreement.

Situation

Cookability Ltd is a UK company that manufactures kitchen equipment, such as food mixers, juice extractors and toasters. The products are sold in the UK and around Europe. The company employs about 5,000 people in a small town, where it is the biggest employer. One of the directors has put forward a proposal to move the manufacturing facility abroad, to a developing country where labour costs are much cheaper.

Role A, in favour of the proposal, turn to page 98.

Role B, partly in favour, turn to page 100.

Role C, mainly against the proposal, turn to page 101.

Role D, completely against the proposal, turn to page 104.

Analysis
5 minutes

Did everybody participate equally in the discussion?
Did you understand the other participants' points of view?
Can you make some positive comments about the way other group members contributed to the discussion?
Was there anything you or other group members could have done to make the discussion more effective?

Self-assessment

Think about your performance on the tasks. Were you able to:

– put your point of view?	☐ yes	☐ need more practice
– listen and take turns?	☐ yes	☐ need more practice
– make your case and respond?	☐ yes	☐ need more practice

Writing 4 Formal correspondence

| Reply to an enquiry | Apologise and give reasons |

26 August 2004

Trevor Jackson
Apex Finance plc
Apex House
Channel Port
Sussex BN35 2XX

a Dear Mr Jackson

b **Proposal for IT maintenance contract***

c Thank you for an excellent meeting on Friday.

d As promised, I enclose** our proposal for your IT maintenance contract.

e Please let me know if you have any questions.

f I look forward to hearing from you.

g Yours sincerely

h Sandra Gavlas
Business Manager

1 Read this letter to a customer. Match each section of the letter a–h with its description 1–8.

1 Subject line
2 Offer to be helpful
3 Name and title
4 Formal greeting
5 Refer to future contact
6 Formal ending
7 Refer to previous contact / correspondence
8 Refer to enclosure / attachment

* A subject line in this position is only necessary in letters sent by post

** Use *enclose* for letters sent by post; use *attach* for emails.

Task 1 **Objective: Reply to enquiry**

You work for A-1 Training. You receive the following enquiry. Write a reply using the same structure as above. Include the points given in the notes.

Dear Sir

I am interested in the IT training courses you offer, as advertised in *Training Monthly*.

Could you please send me a copy of your course programme for this year? My postal address is given above.

Many thanks

Don Bradshaw

Notes

Enclose programme.
Details of company: established training company, 30 years' experience, train IT professionals in latest technology.
Say we can offer advice on selecting the right course.
Give direct phone number.

What do you write?

The phrases below are from an email to a customer about their order. Put the phrases in the correct sequence to create the email.

- ☐ We have items A24 and B39 in stock ...
- ☐ ... due to a high demand for this product at the present time.
- ☐ Dear Ms Bundy
- ☐ We hope to receive new supplies within the next 7–10 days.
- ☐ ... and you should receive them in 2–3 days.
- ☐ We apologise for any inconvenience this may cause.
- ☐ We regret that we are out of stock of item C21 ...
- ☐ Thank you for your order dated March 30.
- ☐ Yours sincerely
- ☐ We will dispatch your order as soon as possible after that.

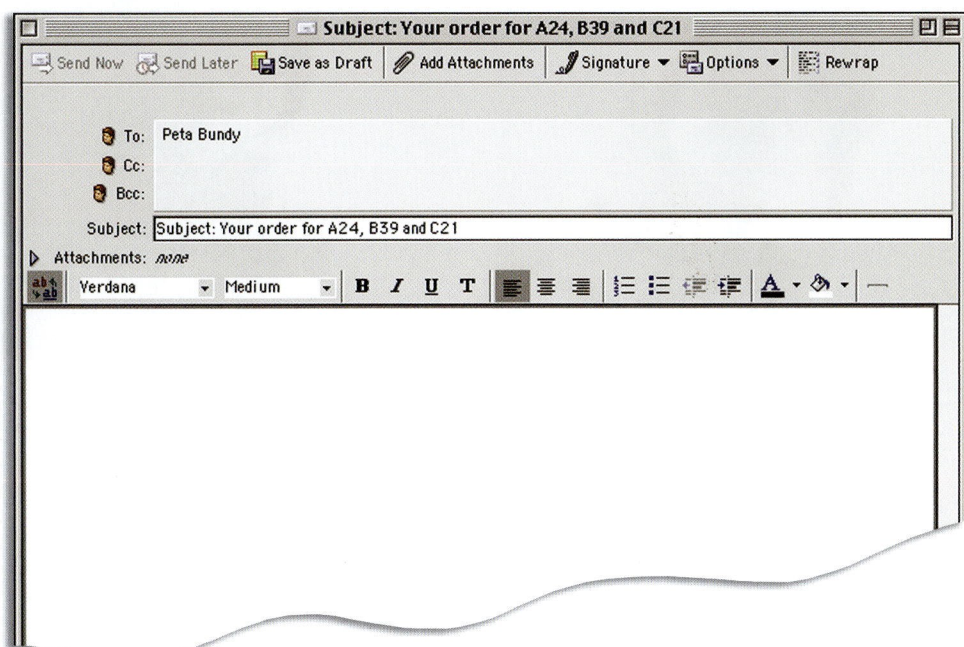

Grammar reference: Gerunds and infinitives, page 96

Task 2

Objective: Apologise and give reasons

You work for a training organisation. Read the brief and write a letter of apology.

Your company is offering a workshop on Building Customer Confidence on June 6th. The maximum number of participants is 35. (You set this limit because you want the workshop to be as interactive as possible.) You have received applications from 40 people. Compose a letter to the last 5 applicants explaining that the workshop is fully booked. Because of its popularity, you plan to hold another similar workshop later in the year. You will inform about the date when you know it. Give your apologies. Say that you will let them know if there are any cancellations.

Unit 13 Lead a meeting

Summarise main points | Encourage people to speak | Control the meeting

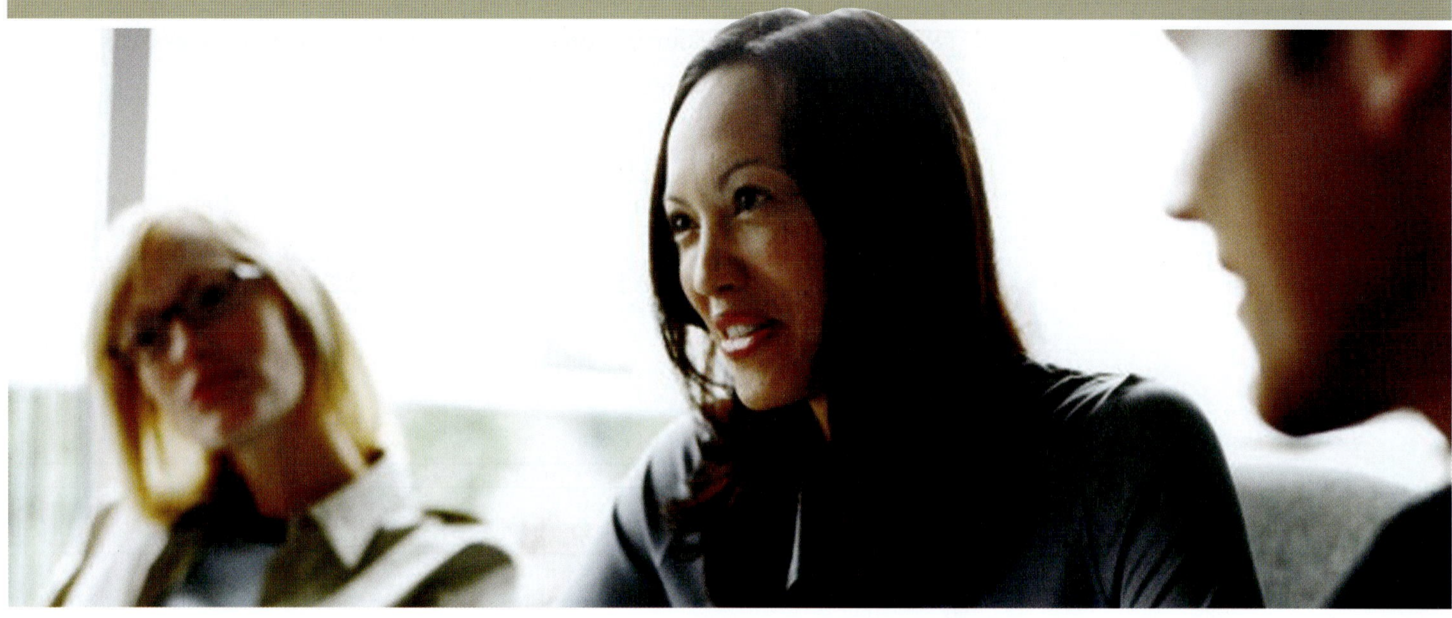

What do you think?
5 minutes

Discuss the role of a leader in meetings. What is the leader responsible for? What should he or she do?

Task 1
Groups of about 4
10 minutes

Objective: Summarise main points

In each group, one person should be ready to summarise the main points from the discussion about the role of a leader. You can take notes if you like. The person responsible for summarising should now report what was said.

You may want to use some of the following language.

The important point is …
The main thing is …
Basically, what they said was …
(Name) thinks that …
But other people said that …
Everybody agreed that …

Analysis
5 minutes

Did the summarisers manage to follow what was said?
Did they summarise the main points accurately?
Did they miss anything?

Grammar reference: Reported speech, page 97

Good business practice, page 79

CD 18 Listening
10 minutes

Listen to six short extracts from a meeting. The group is trying to decide whether to hold their next sales team meeting in the office or in a hotel. What did the leader do in each situation? Match each extract with one of the following actions a–f.

Actions	Extract
a Tell a speaker to keep to the topic.	☐
b Clarify the meaning.	☐
c Encourage someone to say more.	☐
d Summarise.	☐
e Ask someone to contribute.	☐
f Stop one speaker so that another person can speak.	☐

What do you say?
5 minutes

Leading meetings

Match the following phrases 1–6 with an action a–f from the Listening. What other phrases do you know that match each action?

Language	Action
1 OK, Thank you, Jenny. Gaby – you wanted to say something ...	
2 Right. Why do you think that?	
3 Peter – what do you think?	
4 So – to sum up ...	
5 I don't think that belongs to the present discussion.	
6 So, what you're saying is ... , is that right?	

Task 2
Groups of 3–4
15 minutes

Objective: Encourage people to speak

Hold a mini meeting to discuss each topic below. Take it in turns to be leader. The leader should encourage everybody to contribute ideas and summarise the main points after the discussion (See Task 1).

Topics

1 When you have an all-day meeting, is it better to break for lunch or to have sandwiches brought to the meeting room?

2 You want to hold a farewell party for one of your colleagues who is leaving. Should you hold the party in office hours or in the evening?

3 Your meetings are often interrupted by mobile phone calls (sometimes from customers). Should everyone switch off their mobiles during meetings?

Culture at work

Attitudes to interruptions

In some cultures, people like to work in a sequential manner, finishing one task before starting the next. Such people dislike being interrupted in the middle of a task and having to consider something else. In other cultures, people can happily handle several tasks at once. This means they don't mind interruptions. These different attitudes can affect the way meetings are run. How would you describe your culture? How are meetings run in your company/ country? Complete your culture profile on page 82.

	One task at a time	Several tasks at once
Punctuality	Meetings start and finish at specified times. Lateness is not tolerated.	Lateness can be tolerated if there are good reasons.
Agenda	The meeting must follow the agenda. Any changes should be agreed at the start. The leader sometimes sets a time limit for each agenda point.	It may be difficult to follow the agenda exactly. It is considered more important for individuals to be able to talk freely about their various concerns.
Organisation	The meeting is tightly controlled. Interruptions (e.g. phone calls) are not welcomed. Speakers are reminded to keep to the point.	Meetings are more fluid. Interruptions are viewed as normal. Leaders often allow digressions and 'meetings within meetings'.

Task 2
Groups of 3–4
10 minutes
per meeting

Objective: Control the meeting

For each situation below, appoint a different person as leader. Hold a mini meeting and try to reach a decision.

Situations

1 You belong to a team of 12, which holds weekly meetings. The purpose of the meetings is to keep everyone informed of progress and developments. The normal practice is to take turns to lead. You all feel dissatisfied that your meetings take too long and are not well-organised. Discuss how to make them more efficient.

2 You work in an international team which meets once a month. It means travelling between Sweden, Singapore and the USA. Discuss whether it would be better to use video conferencing for meetings.

3 Your team works very well together, but you are not so good at communicating with other people in the company. You need to be better at keeping others informed of what you are doing. You also need to be more aware of what other teams are doing. Hold a meeting to discuss how you can improve the flow of information.

4 You all work for Noll Edge Ltd., a small consulting company. Long-serving staff have a great deal of expertise and experience. New staff joining Noll Edge have excellent qualifications but don't know the business or its customers. How can you encourage the experienced staff to share their knowledge with the newcomers?

Analysis
5 minutes

How did each leader perform?
Did they encourage everyone to speak?
Did they summarise what was said accurately?
Did they keep control effectively?

Self-assessment

Think about your performance on the tasks. Were you able to:

– listen and summarise?	☐ yes	☐ need more practice
– encourage people to speak?	☐ yes	☐ need more practice
– control the meeting?	☐ yes	☐ need more practice

Unit 14 Conclude a presentation

| Make a strong conclusion | Ask questions | Deal with questions |

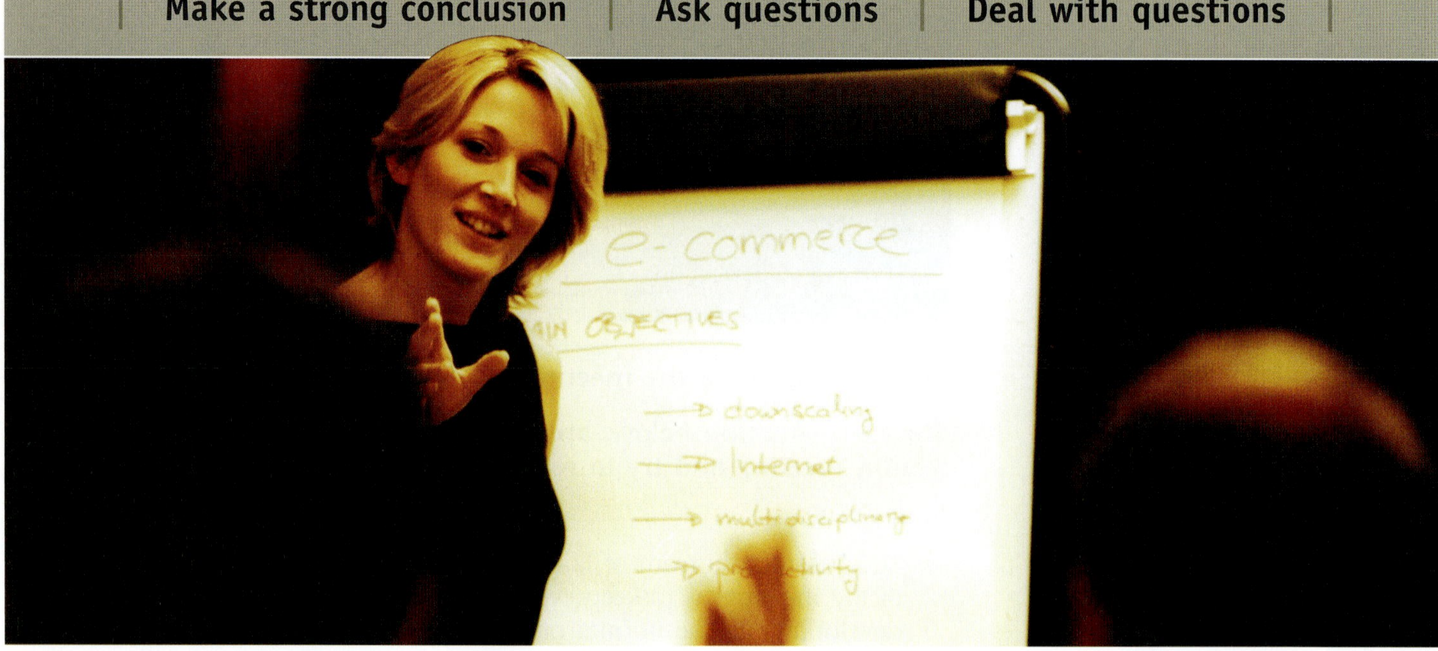

Ending a presentation

What do you think?
Pairs
5 minutes

Match the expressions with the tips on ending a presentation.

1	End as quickly as possible	a	'Do you have any questions?'
2	Make a strong final statement	b	'Oh, I forgot to say that ... '
3	Ask for questions	c	'I'll just explain again ... '
4	Thank the audience for listening	d	'Well, I think that's all I have to say.'
5	Add something new	e	'Thank you for your attention.'
6	Summarise the main points	f	'My conclusion is ... '
7	Explain details again	g	'So to sum up ... '
8	Signal that you are coming to the end	h	'Well that was my final point. So I'll just give you a brief summary.'

Good business practice, page 77

CD 19 Listening 1
10 minutes

A director of Switchett Ltd., a small electronics manufacturing company, makes a presentation to the board about whether to outsource their distribution or build their own warehouse. Listen to the final part of the presentation and answer the questions.

1 Which of the steps above are included, and in what order?

2 a How did the presenter introduce the summary of the presentation?
  b What phrase did he use to refer to the two main points?
  c What phrase did he use to refer back to the results?

3 a What was the main conclusion?
  b What phrase was used to introduce this conclusion?
  c How did the presenter begin his final sentence?

Task 1
Pairs
25 minutes

Objective: Make a strong conclusion

Your company wants to build a new warehouse. Two possible sites for the warehouse have been researched; see the main points below.

Step 1 Preparation

Read your role and information about the site. Prepare the summary and conclusion for a presentation to managers about the two sites.

Partner A: You prefer Site A because of lower cost and close proximity to your factory.

Partner B: You prefer Site B because of its convenient access and no worries about environmental problems.

COMPARISON OF SITES FOR THE NEW WAREHOUSE

	Site A	Site B
Type of site	Brownfield site in an industrial zone Land was previously occupied by chemicals plant (now demolished)	Greenfield site: area not so far developed Land was previously farmland
Access by road	Via small roads A lot of local traffic from other plants in area	Easy access to a major motorway
Proximity to factory	3 kilometres from the factory	35 kilometres from the factory
Cost of land	€500,000	€800,000

Step 2 Presentation

Present your conclusion to your partner.

Analysis
5 minutes

Did your partner summarise all the important points?
How effective was each conclusion?
Did your partner speak strongly and clearly and emphasise key words?

CD 20 Listening 2
10 minutes

Following the presentation in Listening 1, four members of the audience ask questions.

1 Listen and write down the four questions you hear.
2 Match each of the questions with one of the problems a–d.
   a The presenter doesn't know the answer. Question ______
   b The presenter didn't understand the question. Question ______
   c The questioner challenges the presenter's conclusion. Question ______
   d It would take too long to answer. Question ______
3 Listen again. How did the presenter deal with each problem? What did he say?

Task 2
Pairs or small groups
10 minutes

Objective: Ask questions

Step 1

If you were partner A in Task 1, work with another partner A. Partner B, work with another partner B.

Refer to the conclusion your partner in Task 1 presented to you. Prepare six questions for that partner about the site he / she favours. Your questions may request explanations or more details. Try to focus on the following issues.

- recruitment of workers locally
- environmental problems
- security problems in the area
- government plans for other development in the area
- transport costs
- other possible costs

Whole group
5 minutes

Step 2

Compare your questions with those of other pairs. Which questions do you think will be most challenging for the presenter?

Grammar reference: Questions, page 86

What do you say?
5 minutes

Dealing with questions

Here are some typical problems presenters have when dealing with questions. Match each response a–f with a problem 1–6.

Problem

1 You didn't hear the question.
2 You didn't quite understand the question.
3 You don't know the answer.
4 It's a difficult question and you need time to think.
5 The questioner puts a strong argument against your point of view.
6 The question isn't relevant and time is running out.

Response

a I'm not sure about that, but I can find out for you.
b Sorry. I don't think we have time to go into that. Perhaps we can discuss it later.
c That's an interesting question. Let me think ...
d Sorry, are you asking about ... ?
e Sorry, I didn't catch that. Can you repeat the question please?
f That's a good point. However, ...

Good business practice, page 77

Culture at work

Attitudes to critical questions

In some cultures, any public criticism is seen as an insult and must be avoided. In other cultures, it is important to speak the truth, and critical remarks are not taken personally. How would you describe your culture? Complete your culture profile on page 82.

	Criticism is acceptable	Criticism is insulting
Personal involvement	Negative questions or comments are not taken personally.	Any suggestion of disagreement is seen as a personal attack.
Saying what you think	It is important to say what you really think, even if your opinion is negative.	People hide negative opinions and make only mild or positive comments.
Showing disagreement	It is acceptable to ask challenging or hostile questions.	Only polite, safe questions can be asked.

Task 3
Same pairs as Task 1
10 minutes

Objective: Deal with questions

Work with your partner from Task 1. Ask the questions you prepared in Task 2 and any other questions you like. Answer your partner's questions, using the strategies and language from *What do you say?*

To answer questions on site A, turn to page 99.

To answer questions on site B, turn to page 101.

Analysis
5 minutes

Did your partner answer your questions clearly and politely?
Did he / she deal effectively with any difficult questions?

Self-assessment

Think about your performance on the tasks. Were you able to:

- make a strong conclusion? ☐ yes ☐ need more practice
- ask questions? ☐ yes ☐ need more practice
- deal with questions? ☐ yes ☐ need more practice

Unit 15 Celebrate success

| Conclude a deal | Review achievement | Celebrate the conclusion |

Task 1
Groups of 4
40 minutes

Objective: Conclude a deal

Read negotiating situations 1 and 2 below. For situation 1, two people should negotiate a deal and the other two should observe. Switch roles for situation 2.

You have 5 minutes to decide on your target for the negotiation and prepare arguments. Each pair then has about 15 minutes to negotiate and reach agreement.

OK – It's a deal!   Right – I agree!   Good – We have an agreement!

Situation 1

Partner A: You are an inventor with designs for a new and exciting product. You have no capital to produce the product yourself.

Partner B: You are a manufacturing company, Haggler & Co., that wants to produce and sell this product.

The product life span is predicted to be about three years.

You have the following three possibilities for a deal between you.

1 Haggler & Co. pays a fixed price of €200K. The inventor gets no further income from sales.

2 The inventor gets a ten per cent share of profits. If sales are low (20,000 units per year), this would provide an annual income of €40K for the inventor. But sales could be as high as 100,000 units per year, providing an annual income of €200K for the inventor.

3 You could negotiate a combination of 1 and 2.

Situation 2

Partner C: You are a consultant with valuable expertise. Your usual fee is €300 per hour.

Partner D: You are a company, Barters Group, that needs the consultancy skills of Partner C for a specific project. You have a budget for the consultancy work of €12,000. The amount of work is estimated at 30 to 45 hours. However, there is a small chance that it could be more than 50 hours.

You have the following three possibilities for a deal between you.

1 Barters Group will pay a lump sum for the work.

2 The consultant will receive a fee based on the number of hours worked.

3 You could negotiate a combination of 1 and 2.

Observers should make notes on the following.

Who used the most persuasive arguments?
Who got the best deal?
Who could have won a better deal?

Task 2
Whole group
15 minutes

Objective: Review achievement

The observers for each situation in Task 1 should now give their feedback. You may want to use some of the following language.

Positive	Negative
It was a very successful negotiation.	*I'm disappointed that you didn't ...*
I'm impressed with the way you ...	*You could have ...*
One thing you did really well was ...	*I don't think you should have ...*

Grammar reference: Past modals, Page 90

Culture at work

Giving praise

In some cultures, it is usual to praise or reward **individuals** for their personal achievements at work. In other cultures, praise must be given to the **whole group** or team who achieved success by working together. How would you describe your culture? Complete your culture profile on page 82.

	Individual praise	Group praise
Individual feelings	It is acceptable to single out an individual for special praise: the person chosen feels proud.	Showing favouritism is avoided: the person chosen feels embarrassed.
Bonuses	Pay rewards and even promotion are given for individual success.	Rewards or bonuses are shared amongst the group.
Motivation	Individuals are motivated to work for personal achievement.	People are motivated by the strong morale of the team.
I or we?	People say, 'I did this.'	People say, 'We did this.'

What do you think?
Whole group
5 minutes

Concluding the deal

1 What usually happens at the end of a negotiation?

☐ You all shake hands.
☐ You make a verbal summary of what you have agreed.
☐ You prepare minutes of the meeting and send them to the other party within one or two days.
☐ Both parties sign a formal written agreement.

2 Do you usually celebrate the conclusion of a successful negotiation? If so, how do you celebrate?

☐ A party in the office
☐ Lunch in the office restaurant
☐ Dinner at an expensive city restaurant
☐ Go out to a bar or nightclub
☐ Other (give examples): ______________________________

Good business practice, page 81

CD 21 Listening
10 minutes

Listen to the conclusion of a negotiation about a joint venture between Jon Harvey, the inventor of a new interactive toy, and Fabrox, a company that will manufacture the product. Daniel Gascoigne, managing director of Fabrox, chairs the meeting.

a What steps are taken to conclude the deal?
b How are they going to celebrate the success of the negotiation?
c What expressions do they use to show positive feelings about their future relationship?

What do you say?
5 minutes

Celebrating success

Match each sentence a–j with a function 1–5. There are two examples for each function.

1 Thank people
2 Praise people
3 Show appreciation
4 Make a toast
5 Offer good wishes

a You've done a fantastic / excellent / brilliant job!
b I've really enjoyed working with you.
c It's been very productive / useful / interesting.
d Here's to our success in the future!
e Well done!
f Thanks very much for your help!
g I'd like to thank you for all your hard work.
h Good luck with everything.
i I'd like to propose a toast to a long and fruitful partnership between us.
j I hope it all goes well!

Task 3

Objective: Celebrate the conclusion

Individually
10 minutes

Part 1 Propose a toast

Prepare a short toast to conclude your course. You may want to toast your teacher, your fellow course participants or your future success.

Each person should then stand up and propose their toast.

Whole group
5–10 minutes

Part 2 Say goodbye

Walk round the room and say goodbye to each person. When saying goodbye, you should say something positive to the other person, for example, that you have enjoyed working with them. You may show appreciation for something they have done or praise them for something they have achieved. You should end with some good wishes for the future.

Self-assessment

Think about your performance on the tasks. Were you able to:

- conclude a deal? ☐ yes ☐ need more practice
- review achievement? ☐ yes ☐ need more practice
- celebrate the conclusion? ☐ yes ☐ need more practice

Writing 5 Minutes

| Start and end minutes | Record decisions and action points |

What do you think? **Read the pairs of examples and identify which is more formal (F) or more informal (I).**

Headlines

❑ Minutes
DCE Meeting
June 14th

❑ Minutes of the marketing group meeting held on October 25th at 08:30, in room 1410

Who was at the meeting:

❑ Participants: AB, CF, DJ

❑ Present: Muriel Peters (Chair)
Roger Castle (General Manager)
Phillip Payne (Company Secretary)
Board members: Lisa Tomas, Hannah Bloom, George Pulenck ...
Apologies were received from: Isla McGregor, Barry Gardiner

First agenda point

❑ 1 Minutes of previous meeting
The minutes of the previous meeting were approved and signed by the Chair.
2 Matters arising
There has been no action on monthly reports. Reports are being sent quarterly as before. It was agreed that reports would be sent monthly starting from next month.

❑ Reviewed action list from previous meeting.
No action yet on monthly reports. Monthly reporting will start from next month.

Ending

❑ **AOB** Procedure for claiming expenses will be reviewed.
JD to send a memo to all before next meeting.

❑ **Any other business**
GM enquired about expenses. The procedure for claiming expenses will be reviewed and a memo sent to all before the next meeting.

Date of next meeting: 5th July at 10:00

What do you write?

1 Read the following two examples of recording decisions and action points. Underline the words in the formal version that are omitted in the informal one.

A More formal

Point 4: Stationery supplier

As our existing stationery supplier can no longer deliver in our area, it was agreed that we need to identify a new supplier before the end of January. Three quotes from different suppliers are needed. A decision will be taken at the next meeting.

Action: Duncan Smith **Deadline: 20th January**

B Informal

4 New stationery supplier: Our existing supplier can no longer deliver in our area. Need to identify new supplier before end of January. Decision next meeting.
* Duncan to get three quotes by 20th.*

Grammar reference: Passives, page 91

2 Look at the extract from minutes taken at a project team meeting. Re-write the action points in the same way as either A or B above. Re-write all the sentences that are in *italic script*.

2. 2 Travel budget

Roger presented the figures for the last quarter and pointed out that some team members had exceeded their spending limits. This will make it difficult to keep the total annual expenditure within the budget. In order to plan more effectively in future, *it was decided that Maria would create a chart with the names and numbers of business trips planned before the end of the year. This information can be passed to Roger who will revise the budget for the final quarter. Project team members are requested to inform Maria via email of any trips she might not know about. The deadline for the new budget is 25th September.*

2.3 Training

Flavia commented that it was difficult to choose between the many different training programmes that are available. *It was agreed that those who have attended training should write a short report on their experience and distribute it to other team members. Isabel will be responsible for reminding people to prepare and distribute reports.*

Task 1

Objective: Record decisions and action points

Write the minutes of your own meeting

Write one set of minutes for the mini meetings you held in Unit 13, Task 3. Treat each situation as one agenda point.

Good business practice

Presentations

Unit 3 Making an effective presentation

An effective presentation:

- is relevant to the audience and tells them what they need to know.
- is clear and easy to follow.
- has an introduction in which the objectives are made clear.
- has a clearly-defined structure with three or four main points.
- is usually accompanied by helpful visuals.
- ends with a strong summary.
- fits the time schedule.

Unit 3 Preparing a presentation

- Start by thinking about your audience: who they are and what they want to know. Make a structured plan for your talk.

Do	Don't
– Write the introduction so that you can make a clear and confident start.	– Don't try to write the whole presentation word by word: it is more difficult to understand someone reading aloud from a script.
– Prepare a few visuals to save words and illustrate what you want to say.	– Don't use too many visuals – about one for each minute of talking time is enough.
– Keep the visuals simple: make sure information is large and clear.	– Don't make visuals too complex or give too many details.
– Try to use colour and add some pictures to your visuals.	– Don't include too much text or too many figures.

Unit 8 Delivering a presentation

- Remember to face the audience and make eye contact with them.
- Speak clearly and fairly slowly.
- Use simple language with short sentences.
- Emphasise key words and pause briefly between points.
- Repeat key numbers or write them on a visual.
- Involve the audience by asking a question from time to time.

Unit 6 Using visuals in a presentation

Which equipment?

☐ **Flipchart:**
- useful for informal and interactive talks
- you need to have good handwriting

☐ **Overhead projector:**
- useful with large and small audiences
- you need time to prepare good transparencies

☐ **Digital projector:**
- useful in any situation
- easy to prepare visuals on your PC or laptop
- good for colour pictures and animations

Presenting visuals:
- Make sure the audience can see each visual clearly.
- Give the audience enough time to see each visual.
- Help the audience to understand the visuals by pointing to parts you are referring to.
- Don't turn your back on the audience to look at the visual.
- Don't read the text on your visuals word for word.

Unit 10 Presenting an effective argument

- Present your proposal in a logical way: people react positively to ideas that are well organised.
- Emphasise the benefits of your proposal.
- Use *we* rather than *I* or *you* to get support from others.
- Choose two or three strong arguments: too many reasons can weaken your case.
- Be positive: say what you want, not what you don't want.
- When presenting a detailed argument, use facts and figures to support your ideas.

Unit 14 Ending a presentation

- If you signal to the audience that you are coming to the end, you will then have their full attention.
- Summarise each of the main points.
- Make a short but strong conclusion.
- Prepare the final sentence of your talk beforehand, and practise saying it clearly and strongly.

Unit 14 Dealing with questions

- Anticipate the questions and prepare some answers beforehand.
- Make sure the audience has heard the question: it is useful to repeat it.
- Address answers to the whole audience, not just to the questioner.
- Be honest if you don't know the answer.
- Never get into an argument with the questioner.

Meetings

Unit 4 Opening a meeting

It is important to state the purpose of a meeting in the introduction. The introduction normally includes five stages:

1 Signal the start of the meeting (if there are a number of participants).

2 Greet and welcome participants; introduce any new participants.

3 Explain the background to the meeting.

4 State the purpose of the meeting.

5 Ask for contributions or hand over to the first speaker.

In formal meetings, there may be a sixth stage in which you set the protocol for the meeting, for example, appoint someone to take minutes, agree the time limit or say whether contributions should be made through the leader.

Unit 7 Holding a brainstorming meeting

The purpose of a brainstorming meeting is to generate as many ideas as possible, then to produce a short list of ideas and finally to agree on the best idea and action plan. The following points are important.

- Three to eight people is an ideal number for brainstorming meetings.
- People think more creatively in a relaxed atmosphere.
- It is useful to have a facilitator who does not contribute, but keeps the session on course and records ideas.
- Everyone should feel that their opinions are valued.
- Do not reject any ideas during brainstorming. Criticism kills creativity.
- Don't judge or analyse ideas during brainstorming.
- Write all ideas on a board or flipchart.
- When enough ideas have been suggested, make a short list of the best ones.
- When you have finished brainstorming, evaluate the ideas by considering how they would work in practice.

Unit 12 Participating in meetings

The following points are important to help make a meeting more effective and to achieve your own objectives.

- Prepare thoroughly for the meeting.
- Know your own objectives before the meeting starts.
- Speak clearly and confidently when making your point.
- Show respect by listening carefully to others.
- It takes time to develop an argument: allow other speakers to make their points clear.
- Adapt your contribution to reflect what others have said.
- Be able to concede a point if you are wrong.
- Remember that you share a common purpose with others at the meeting.

Unit 13 Leading a meeting

To help a meeting be more efficient, the leader should:

- take care of practical matters (introduce participants, decide who will take minutes).
- set and keep the rules of the meeting.
- follow the agenda.
- bring matters to a conclusion.
- assign actions.

Time-keeping is important. The leader should:

- start on time.
- keep the discussion on the point.
- keep to time limits.

The leader should control the discussion and:

- make sure everyone has the chance to express their viewpoint.
- clarify anything that may be unclear.
- listen.
- summarise the discussion clearly at regular intervals.
- deal with conflicts.

Larger meetings are more effective if:

- only one person speaks at a time.
- the leader decides who should speak.

Unit 2 Getting things done on time

Whether you are planning a special project or simply organising your routine working day, the following steps can help you to meet your deadlines and stay in control

Do

- Make a list of tasks (things you must achieve).
- Break down the tasks into shorter steps or actions.
- Set a deadline for completing each action.
- Do the most urgent tasks first.
- Predict and try to prevent problems.
- Check your list regularly and make sure you are on track to meet your deadlines.

Don't

- Don't put off tasks because they are difficult or you don't like them.
- Don't concentrate too much on one task and forget all the others.

Telephoning

Unit 5 Telephoning problems

Many people nowadays avoid the telephone and prefer to send emails instead. But calling is more effective in a number of situations: dealing with urgent problems, getting an immediate response, discussions and joint decision-making and making personal contact with your business partners.

Before making a call:

- Ask yourself: What is the purpose of this call?
- Ask yourself: Who am I going to speak to? What do they need to know? How can they help me?
- Prepare what you want to say.
- Predict any problems you could have (e.g. the person you want isn't there).

During the call:

- Speak clearly and check that the other person understands you.
- Don't let the other person rush you.
- Respond frequently (saying: yes, mm, OK) so the other person knows you are still there.
- Make notes during the call.
- Check that you have understood correctly.
- Repeat important information, especially names and numbers.
- Confirm any arrangements.
- Always be polite and friendly.
- Smile while talking.

After the call:

- Send an email to confirm what you said.

Socialising

Unit 1 Meeting new business partners

The first few seconds of a first meeting are the most important, so it is vital to create the right impression.

- Dress appropriately (it is better to be conservative).
- Check your appearance just before you meet.
- Greet your partners in a warm and friendly manner.
- Introduce everyone who is present, or have them introduce themselves.
- Speak clearly, especially when giving important information.
- Remember that foreign names are often difficult to catch.
- Show interest in the other person by making eye contact when they are speaking.
- Try to relax – taking a slow deep breath can help.

Unit 9 Good business relations

To develop a mutual understanding with your business partners, it will be important to devote some time to getting to know them through small talk and conversation.

- Be aware of how important small talk is in the cultures you do business with.
- If you find small talk difficult, prepare some topics before the meeting.
- Avoid topics that could arouse strong feelings (e.g. politics and religion).
- Prepare some questions; use open questions (What? Where? How?).
- Listen and respond to the other person – don't talk too much!
- Even if the meeting is difficult, always stay calm and polite.
- After the meeting, say a warm goodbye and talk about the next contact.

Negotiating

Unit 11 Negotiation strategies

- Prepare carefully: be clear about what you want.
- Build good rapport with the other person.
- Find out what the other person wants so you can offer them benefits.
- Use reasons and arguments to support your proposals.
- Try to find ways to agree.
- Be creative: look for alternative solutions.

If someone makes you an offer you don't want to agree to, you can use the following strategies to respond in a way that keeps the door open and avoids conflict.

- Avoid giving an immediate reaction.
- Don't be afraid to stay silent.
- Summarise to clarify that you've understood.
- Ask questions to find out more about the other person's position.
- Take a break to give yourself time to think.
- Propose an alternative.

Unit 15 Concluding a negotiation

It is important to:

- summarise orally to make sure everyone understands and nothing is ambiguous.
- build deadlines and a schedule for implementation into your agreement.

When you have successfully negotiated an agreement:

- react positively and enthusiastically.
- smile, shake hands and congratulate each other warmly.

After the meeting:

- summarise what you have agreed in writing or write up minutes of your meeting.
- circulate your summary or minutes as soon as possible after the meeting.

Culture profile

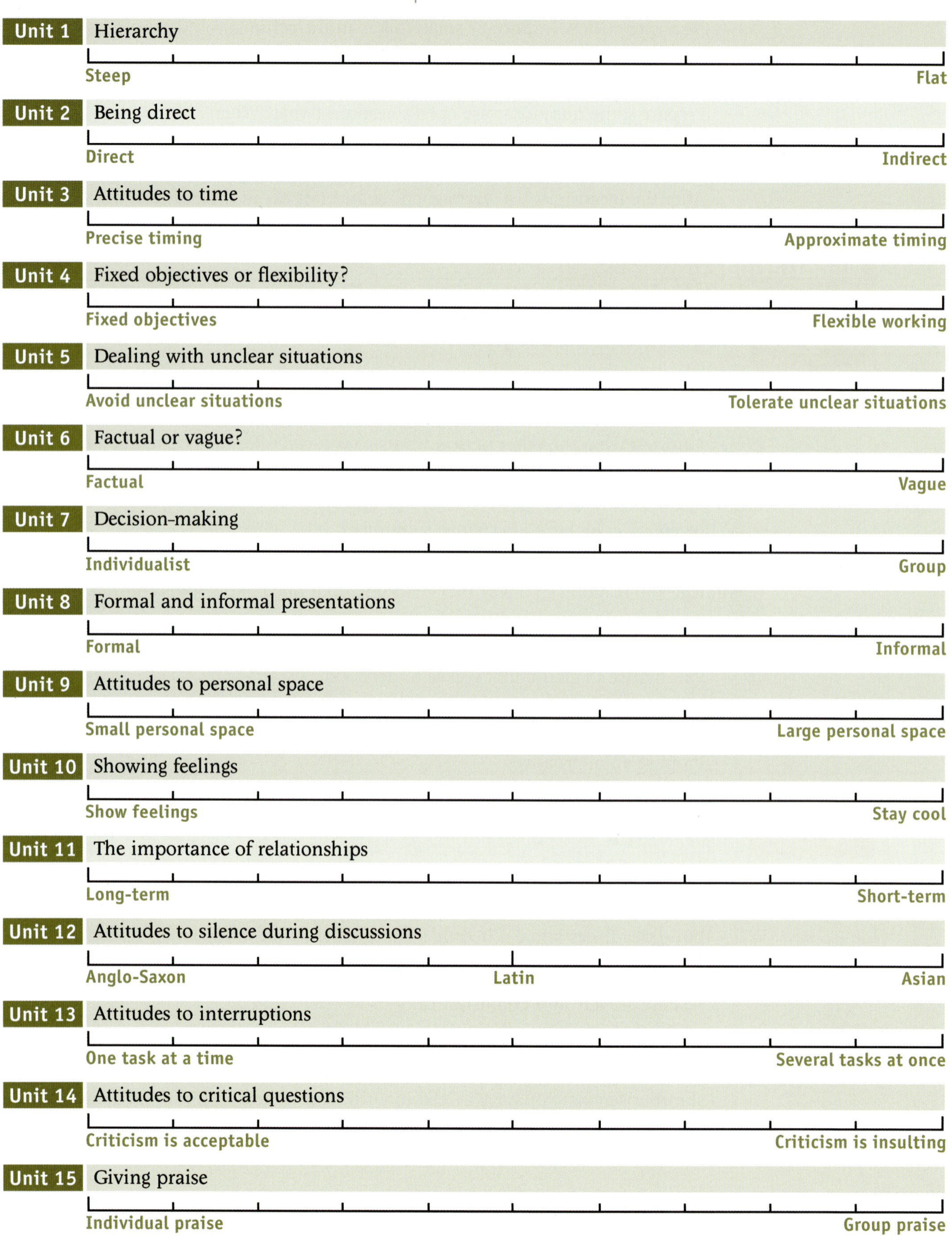
Unit 1 Hierarchy
Steep
Flat
Unit 2 Being direct
Direct
Indirect
Unit 3 Attitudes to time
Precise timing
Approximate timing
Unit 4 Fixed objectives or flexibility?
Fixed objectives
Flexible working
Unit 5 Dealing with unclear situations
Avoid unclear situations
Tolerate unclear situations
Unit 6 Factual or vague?
Factual
Vague
Unit 7 Decision-making
Individualist
Group
Unit 8 Formal and informal presentations
Formal
Informal
Unit 9 Attitudes to personal space
Small personal space
Large personal space
Unit 10 Showing feelings
Show feelings
Stay cool
Unit 11 The importance of relationships
Long-term
Short-term
Unit 12 Attitudes to silence during discussions
Anglo-Saxon
Latin
Asian
Unit 13 Attitudes to interruptions
One task at a time
Several tasks at once
Unit 14 Attitudes to critical questions
Criticism is acceptable
Criticism is insulting
Unit 15 Giving praise
Individual praise
Group praise

Grammar reference

Present simple and continuous

The present simple has the following uses.

- regular events and processes
  We ***hold*** *four meetings a year.*
  We ***don't*** *usually* ***start*** *till 9 o'clock.*
  How often ***do*** *you* ***travel*** *on business?*

Key words

a week / month / year, always, ever, never, often, rarely, seldom, sometimes, usually

- facts that will not change
  Our company ***manufactures*** *mobile phones.*
  Where ***do*** *you* ***export*** *to?*
  I ***don't take*** *sugar in coffee.*
- timetables and scheduled events
  When ***does*** *the plane* ***leave****?*
  The conference ***starts*** *at 9:30 am.*

The present continuous has the following uses.

- events happening now
  I'm working *on a project to promote sales.*
  Our sales ***are growing*** *fast.*
  Are *you* ***enjoying*** *your new job?*

Key words

now, at the moment, currently

- temporary situations
  *We****'re attending*** *a training course this week.*
  I'm not working *at head office at the moment.*
  Are *you* ***staying*** *at the new hotel?*
- future arrangements
  Where ***are*** *we* ***meeting*** *on Friday?*
  My colleague ***isn't coming*** *to the meeting.*

The continuous is *not* usually used with the following stative verbs.

- verbs that express opinions or feelings
  like, dislike, hate, prefer, want, believe, think, feel, mean, understand, realise, recognise
  *Exception: We****'re thinking*** *about your proposal. (=considering)*
- verbs of the senses
  see, hear, feel, smell, taste, seem
  *Exception: I****'m seeing*** *him tomorrow (=meeting)*
- verbs of ownership
  have, need, want
  Exception: *We****'re having*** *lunch tomorrow.*
  (*have* doesn't indicate ownership)

Exercises

1 Complete the text with the correct form of the verbs in brackets.

I ([1] work) __________ for a company that ([2] make)__________ office furniture.
We ([3] sell)__________ to companies all over Europe, so I often ([4] travel)__________ in my job.
Right now I ([5] plan) __________ a trip to Cyprus, which is a new market for us. I ([6] meet) __________ some prospective distributors there next week. Some people ([7] say) __________ that it's difficult to enter a new market.
But I ([8] not think) __________ it's going to be a problem for us. We ([9] have) __________ good contacts in the region who ([10] know) __________ the local conditions.

2 Look at the underlined verb phrases. Is the verb form correct? If not, correct it.

Hi, Sam

[1] I am needing your help. [2] We're thinking of buying some new equipment. [3] I know [4] you're having some experience of this, and [5] I'm hoping you can give me some advice. [6] We are currently trying out the Servex Multijob X15, which [7] we have on loan from head office, but it's too big for our needs. [8] Servex is also making a smaller model: the X12. Is that the model [9] you are using at the moment? If so, what [10] are you thinking about it? [11] Are you liking it?

Many thanks for you help.

Best regards

Toni

Key to Exercise 1

1 work 2 makes 3 sell 4 travel 5 am planning
6 am meeting 7 say 8 don't think 9 have
10 know

Key to Exercise 2

1 incorrect (I need) 2 correct 3 correct
4 incorrect (you have) 5 correct, 6 correct
7 correct 8 incorrect (makes) 9 correct
10 incorrect (do you think)
11 incorrect (Do you like)

Future forms

will + infinitive has the following uses.

- predictions
  *My talk **will last** about five minutes.*
  ***Will** your team **have** a lot of questions?*
  *We **won't be** able to raise the funds within a month.*
- spontaneous decisions or offers
  *Now **I'll move** on to my next point*
  ***I'll explain** this in more detail later.*
  ***I'll call** you back as soon as I can.*
- things that we want to make happen
  ***I'll finish** everything before I leave on holiday.*
  ***We'll meet** our targets whatever happens.*

going to + verb has the following uses.

- personal intentions
  ***I'm going to cover** three main points.*
  ***Are** you **going to finish** by 12?*
  ***I'm going to study** English in my spare time.*
- predictions
  *Our new product **is going to to be** a big success.*
  *We**'re not going to see** much change in the near future.*

> ***will* or *going to*?**
>
> Often either verb phrase is possible with no change in meaning.
> ***I'll come** back later.*
>
> ***I'm going to come** back to that later.*
>
> However, **will** *usually* has a more spontaneous feel, whereas **going to** suggests present evidence.
> *The figures show that we**'re not going to meet** our target.*
> *We**'ll work** hard to make sure we meet our target.*

Other ways to express the future.

- The present simple is used for timetabled events.
  *The plane **leaves** at 7:30 tomorrow.*
- The present continuous is used for events you have fixed or arranged.
  *We**'re meeting** the suppliers next Monday.*
- Modal verbs can, may and might are used for uncertain predictions.
  *It **could be** difficult to finish by six.*
  *We **might have to** lower the price.*

Exercises

1 Change the underlined verb phrases to an appropriate future form where necessary.

In my presentation this morning, [1] I'm giving you an overview of our plans for the new office building. [2] I'm just outlining the main points briefly and then [3] you have the chance to study the drawings and to ask questions.

OK - so this is the plan.

As you know, [4] we're expanding our staff and we're predicting that [5] we have 1,400 staff altogether by the end of next year. The new building [6] is able to accommodate up to 2,000, so [7] there is plenty of room for further expansion ...

Now [8] I'm just going over the schedule for the move. Ideally, we want to move everyone in by 15th August. However, [9] this is perhaps difficult because of all the building work that [10] we have to complete by then. [11] We're meeting with the builders on Monday and [12] we're trying to get a commitment from them to complete by mid August ...

So, to come back to the schedule. The main building work [13] starts on 1st March and the first stage [14] takes maybe 8 to 10 weeks. This is the stage where [15] we possibly see some delays, because [16] we are dependent on subcontractors and the delivery of materials. But if all goes well, we expect to start the second stage by mid May. [17] That part takes a further ten weeks, which brings us up to the end of July. Then, hopefully, [18] we start the third stage – the internal painting and equipping of the new offices – at the beginning of August.

Key to Exercise 1

1 I'll / I'm going to
2 I'll just outline / I'm just going to
3 you will have 4 we're expanding (no change)
5 we'll have, 6 will be able to, 7 there will be
8 I'll just go over 9 this may be / could be
10 we have to / we will have to
11 we're meeting (no change)
12 we're going to try 13 starts (no change)
14 may / could / might take
15 we may / could / might see
16 we'll be / we're going to be
17 will take / is going to take, 18 we'll start

Present perfect and past simple

The present perfect has the following uses.

- changes that affect the present
  We've ***agreed*** *on four objectives.*
  Have *you* ***re-organised*** *the department?*
  We ***haven't implemented*** *all the changes yet.*
- situations that started in the past and still continue
  I've worked *here for 12 years.*
  The CEO ***has*** *never* ***visited*** *our subsidiary.*
  How long ***have*** *you* ***been*** *in your present job?*
- Note that we can sometimes use the **present perfect continuous** here, especially to emphasise long duration.
  *We****'ve been working*** *here for a long time!*
- recent events.
  The price ***has increased*** *this month.*

Key words

for (with periods of time) and *since* (with points in time: e.g. times, days, dates, etc.); *already, yet, just, ever, never, recently, lately, in the last . . . months / year; today, this week / month / year; how long? how many times?*

The past simple has the following uses.

- finished actions and events
  She ***worked*** *here for five years.* (= She doesn't work here now.)
  Prices ***increased*** *last year.*
- reference to specific times in the past
  I ***joined*** *the company ten years ago.*
  When ***did*** *you last* ***visit*** *the US?*

Key words

last week / month / year;
weeks / months / years ago;
in + month / year; at +o'clock;
on + day; when?

Perfect or past?

- without a time adverbial, the choice of perfect or past can make news sound either very new or old.
  *They****'ve released*** *a new product. (recently)*
  They ***released*** *a new product. (some time ago)*
  *They****'ve introduced*** *a bonus scheme. (news)*
  They ***introduced*** *a bonus scheme. (old news)*

Exercises

1 Complete the dialogue with the correct form of the verbs in brackets.

Leader Good morning everyone. Are we all here?

Bertrand Er, no – Daniela isn't here.

Leader What ([1] happen) ______________ to her?

Bertrand Her assistant ([2] call) ____________ a few minutes ago. Apparently she ([3] have) __________ an accident. She ([4] fall) _____down some stairs earlier this morning and she ([5] have to) __________ go to hospital. They think she ([6] break) _______her ankle.

Alicia How terrible! I hope she'll be OK.

Leader Well, we must make a start. When we ([7] meet) __________ last week, we ([8] decide) ___________ that we ([9] need) ___________ to review the procedure for rewarding good performance. Since then, two of you – that's Philippa and Duncan – ([10] do) __________ some research into several different models which we might consider. Philippa, can we start with you? What ([11] you find) _______ out?

2 Decide if the sentences below contain mistakes. Change the form of the verb where necessary.

1 I'm working in this company since two years.
2 I have been in the US a year ago.
3 I was there for five weeks in 1999.
4 The price has increased several times this month.
5 I was in this job for 30 years.
6 The computer crashed – probably a virus.

Key to Exercise 1

1 has happened 2 called 3 has had 4 fell
5 has had to 6 has broken 7 met 8 decided,
9 need / needed 10 have done
11 have you found out

Key to Exercise 2

1 I've worked / I've been working in this company for two years. 2 I was in / went to 3 correct – no change
4 correct – no change 5 I've been 6 has crashed

Questions

Yes / No questions

- The auxiliary comes before the subject.
  Are you Scottish?
  Can we make a start?
  Does your company export much?
  Did you have any trouble finding us?
  Will you travel back tonight?
  Would you like some coffee?

Open questions

- These start with a question word or words.
  Where is your head office?
  When did you arrive?
  How long have you been in this job?
  What did you do before that?
- If ***who***, ***what***, ***which***, ***how many*** or ***how much*** is the subject of the question, there is no auxiliary.
  Who gave you that brochure?
  How many people work in your department?
- If ***who***, ***what*** or ***which*** is the direct or indirect object of the question and is dependent on a preposition, the preposition comes at the end.
  Who do you export to?
  Which department do you work in?

Polite requests and questions

- These start with a polite phrase. The word order is the same as for a statement.
  ***Could you** tell me where the cloakroom is?*
  ***Would you mind** if I used your phone?*
  ***Do you mind** if I ask how old you are?*

Question tags

- These are used when the questioner knows the answer but wants to encourage conversation or, in meetings and negotiations, to press for commitment.
  *Fiona is Scottish, **isn't she?***
  *You don't eat meat, **do you?***
  *You're happy with the contract, **aren't you?***
  *You'll let us know soon, **won't you?***

Exercises

1 Write the questions for the answers below. The key information is in bold.

1 We're leaving **on Friday at 4 pm.**
2 I'm having dinner **with our Japanese partners.**
3 We employ **6,000 staff.**
4 We've known each other **for six years.**
5 I didn't tell you **because it was confidential.**
6 I recommend **the more expensive model.**
7 It cost **$12,000.**
8 We've decided **not to do anything.**

2 Make these questions more polite.

1 How much are they going to pay you?
2 Where's the accounts department?
3 Can I leave my coat here?
4 What did you pay for your car?
5 What's your name? I can't remember.

3 Add appropriate question tags.

1 You don't know my colleague, Tom?
2 We met last year?
3 You'll phone me when you arrive?
4 You're Jacques Leconte?
5 You weren't on holiday last week?

Key to Exercise 1

1 When are you leaving?
2 Who are you having dinner with?
3 How many staff do you employ?
4 How long have you known each other?
5 Why didn't you tell me?
6 Which model do you recommend?
7 How much did it cost?
8 What did you decide (to do)?

Key to Exercise 2

1 Could you tell me / Would you mind telling me how much they are going to pay you?
2 Could you tell me where the accounts department is?
3 Do you mind if I leave my coat here?
4 Could you tell me / Would you mind telling me what you paid for your car?
5 Could you please tell me your name again?

Key to Exercise 3

1 You don't know my colleague, Tom, do you?
2 We met last year, didn't we?
3 You'll phone me when you arrive, won't you?
4 You're Jacques Leconte, aren't you?
5 You weren't on holiday last week, were you?

Modal verbs, part 1

can, could, would, may, might

Can, could and would have the following uses.

- requests

  ***Can** you help me, please?*

  ***Could** you please send me your comments?*

  ***Would** you ask her to call me?*

  ***Can** I call you at ten?*

  ***Could** we see your calculations?*

- typical responses

  Yes, of course. That's no problem.

  I'm afraid I can't help you.

  That could be rather difficult.

  I'm not sure I'll have time.

- offers and invitations

  ***Can** you join us for lunch?*

  ***Would** your colleague like to come too?*

  ***Could** you come for dinner on Friday?*

- typical responses

  I'd like that very much.

  That would be very nice.

  I'm sorry, I can't.

***Can, could** and **may** are used to express permission.*

***May I/ Could I** make a photocopy of this?*

*You **can** use this phone if you like.*

*I'm afraid you **can't** smoke in here.*

- typical responses

  Of course you can.

  I'm sorry, you can't do that.

Could, may and might are used to express uncertainty.

*There **could** be some delays.*

*It **may** be difficult to find a taxi.*

*We **might** lose the sale.*

- Note that **should** can be used to express **probability.**

  *I **should** be there by midday. (= I expect to be)*

- We use **will** to express **certainty about the future.**

  *I'll definitely **be** late.*

Exercises

1 Choose the best modal verb to complete the dialogue politely.

Alberta (1 Could / Would) you like to come for dinner with us this evening?

Sanjay That (2 could / would) be great! Thanks.

Alberta We're going to the Platinum Restaurant.

Sanjay I'm afraid I don't know it. (3 Can / May) you tell me how to get there?

Alberta We (4 can / may) pick you up from your hotel - say at 7:30?

Sanjay Great! But (5 could / would) you make it 8 o'clock, do you think? I have to make a phone call at 7:30.

Alberta Of course – we (6 can / may) say 8:30 if you like?

Sanjay No – 8 is fine. Er – sorry to ask, but (7 can / could) I smoke in this restaurant?

Alberta I'm afraid not. You (8 can't / couldn't) smoke in any public places in this country.

2 Rewrite the following sentences in this dialogue. Replace all the words in bold, using *could, may, might, should* or *will*.

Gavin 1 **It's possible that** Simone is late today.

Ros Her car has broken down and she's waiting for a mechanic. 2 It **will possibly** take some time. 3 **I expect her** to arrive by 11 o'clock.

Gavin 4 She certainly **isn't going to be** here in time for the meeting – it starts in five minutes!

Ros 5 **It's possible for us to** delay the meeting.

Gavin 6 Yes, but **it's maybe** difficult to warn all the other participants now.

Key to Exercise 1

1 Would, 2 would, 3 Can, 4 can, 5 could
6 can, 7 can, 8 can't

Key to Exercise 2

1 Simone may be late today.
2 It could / may / might take some time.
3 She should arrive by 11 o'clock.
4 She (certainly) won't be here in time for the meeting.
5 We could delay the meeting.
6 it may be difficult to warn ...

Modal verbs, part 2

must, should, need, have to, could

Must, should, need and have to have the following uses.

- obligation, necessity or prohibition

  *We **must** keep this confidential.*

  *You **mustn't** talk about it outside this office.*

  *We **have to** install safety equipment.*

  *We **need to** check the contract very carefully.*
- lack of obligation or necessity

  *We **needn't** finish this today.*

  *You **don't have to** get an import licence.*
- certainty

  *It's in the dictionary so it **must be** correct.*
- recommendations, suggestions and advice

  *We **should** spend more on security.*

  *You **shouldn't** take a decision without consulting your manager.*

  *We **must** act right away. (strong)*
- Note that we use could for polite or tentative suggestions.

  *Perhaps we **could** hire a car.*

  ***Couldn't** you ask your manager to help?*
- formal recommendations

  For formal recommendations (especially in writing), we use these expressions rather than modals.

  We recommend that you increase your expenditure on security.

  We recommend increasing expenditure on security.

  It is recommended that you increase expenditure on security.

  An increase in expenditure on security is strongly recommended.

Exercises

1 Complete the sentences below using an appropriate modal according to the description in brackets: *should/ shouldn't, must/ mustn't, need / needn't, have to / don't have to, could / couldn't.*

1 The regulations state that you _________ bring more than $10,000 into the country. (prohibited)

2 You _________ complete a customs declaration to say how much foreign currency you have with you. (obligation)

3 You ________ declare local currency. (no necessity)

4 You ________ get a receipt for any currency you exchange. (recommended)

5 You ________ have an international driving licence if you want to hire a car. (obligation)

6 You ________ walk around town alone at night. (not recommended)

7 You ________ carry too much cash. (strong advice)

8 If you are robbed, you ________ notify the police within 24 hours. (obligation)

9 You ________ ask the hotel to keep your money in the safe. (polite suggestion)

10 You _________ carry your passport – you can leave it at the hotel. (not necessary)

11 If you carry a camera, people will think you _________ be a tourist. (certainty)

12 _________ you wear some more suitable clothes? (polite suggestion)

2 Write the following as formal recommendations.

Example: Carry a copy of your passport.

Answer: We recommend that you carry a copy of your passport.

1 Take out adequate insurance cover.

2 Check on baggage restrictions before travelling.

3 Consult the embassy about visa requirements.

4 You should have vaccinations against yellow fever and typhoid.

Key to Exercise 1

1 mustn't 2 have to / must, 3 don't have to / needn't 4 should 5 must / have to 6 shouldn't 7 mustn't 8 must 9 could 10 don't have to / needn't 11 must 12 Couldn't

Key to Exercise 2

1 We recommend that you take out adequate insurance cover 2 We recommend that you check on baggage restrictions ... 3 We recommend that you consult ... 4 We recommend that you should have vaccinations ...

Conditionals 1 and 2

Conditional sentences are formed as follows.

- **Type 1:** *if* + present tense, present tense or modal

  If we ***outsource****, we'****ll reduce*** *our costs.*

  If we ***don't do*** *it, we* ***might lose*** *market share.*

- **Type 2:** *if* + past tense, **would / could** + verb

  If we ***reduced*** *costs, we'****d make*** *more profit.*

  Could *we* ***save*** *money if we* ***closed*** *down some outlets?*

Conditional type 1 has the following uses.

- cause and effect

  If you ***criticise*** *people, you'****ll kill*** *their creativity.*

  People ***work*** *harder if you* ***motivate*** *them.*

- predict consequences of likely situations

  Morale ***will fall*** *if we* ***lay*** *people off.*

  *We'****ll lose*** *sales if we* ***don't reduce*** *prices.*

- request action in the event of a likely situation

  Tell *me if you* ***get*** *any new ideas.*

  Let *me know if you* ***want*** *another meeting.*

Conditional type 2 has the following uses.

- predict consequences of unlikely situations

  If sales ***increased*** *by 20 per cent, we'****d have*** *the money to expand.*

- make tentative suggestions

  If we ***invested*** *more in advertising, we* ***could increase*** *sales.*

  It ***might be*** *better if we* ***didn't waste*** *so much time.*

- talk about unreal and hypothetical situations

  If our overheads ***weren't*** *so high, we* ***could invest*** *more.*

  If we ***had*** *more people, we'****d be*** *able to work faster.*

  What ***would*** *you* ***do*** *if you* ***were*** *the boss?*

- in negotiating, an offer linked to a type 2 conditional is useful because it is hypothetical, not definite.

  I'd be *willing to place a bigger order if you* ***offered*** *us a discount.*

  Would *you* ***be*** *interested if we* ***included*** *servicing in the price?*

Exercises

1 Complete the conditional sentences with the correct form of the verb.

1 If we (mail / mailed) it today, you'll get it tomorrow.

2 Please call me if the flight (is / will be) delayed.

3 If we (introduce / introduced) flexitime, people would be more motivated to work harder.

4 If we had more time, (we'll / we'd) be able to prepare some new publicity material.

5 If we (save / saved) money on travel expenses, we could spend more on new equipment.

6 If you (place / placed) an order today, we could offer you a lower price.

7 People (will spend / spent) more if they're feeling relaxed.

8 If we played background music in the store, people (will / would) feel more relaxed.

2 Write the verbs in the appropriate form to make a conditional sentence with the meaning that is given in brackets.

1 If the economy (be)______ stronger, we (have) ______ better growth prospects. (hypothetical)

2 If we (increase)________ our marketing effort, we (improve) __________ sales. (cause and effect)

3 Our competitors (gain)_________ market share if we (not introduce) _________new models soon. (predicting likely situation)

4 Just (send)__________ me an email if you (have) ________ any problems. (request)

5 It (be) __________ better if we (be) ________ honest about the situation. (tentative suggestion)

6 We (be) __________ willing to pay more if you (guarantee) _________ an earlier delivery date. (hypothetical negotiating point)

7 If we (fail) _________ to complete the project on time, we (have to) __________ pay a penalty. (unlikely situation)

Key to Exercise 1

1 mail 2 is 3 introduced 4 we'd 5 saved 6 placed
7 will spend 8 would

Key to Exercise 2

1 was – would have 2 increase – will improve
3 will gain – don't introduce 4 send – have
5 would – were 6 would – guaranteed / could guarantee
7 failed – would have to

Conditional type 3 and past modal forms

Conditional type 3 is formed as follows.

- *If* + *had* + past participle of verb, **would / could have** + past participle of verb
- *If I **had known** about the problem, I **would have done** something.*

  *We'**d have agreed** to your proposal if it **hadn't been** so expensive.*

Conditional type 3 has the following uses.

- evaluate or analyse past actions

  *If we'**d made** the decision sooner, we **could have saved** a lot of money. (= We should have decided sooner.)*

  *If we'**d installed** the cameras last year, we **wouldn't have been** robbed. (= We should have installed the cameras last year.)*
- talk about hypothetical situations in the past

  *I'**d have invited** you for dinner if I **had known** you were free. (But I didn't know.)*

  *If he'**d gone** to university, he **could have got** a better job. (He didn't go to university.)*

Some conditional sentences mix Types 2 and 3.

- *If he'**d gone** to university, he'**d have** a better job now.*

Past modals are formed as follows.

- modal verb + *has* / *have* + past participle of verb

  *I **could have taken** a train.*

  *They **should have left** earlier.*

Past modal verbs have the following uses.

- analyse or evaluate what people have done

  Criticising: *You **should have tried** harder*

  *You **shouldn't have wasted** so much time.*

  *You **could have asked** for help.*

  Praising: *You **couldn't have done** anything more.*
- talk about alternative possibilities

  *With more time, we **could have got** a better result.*

  *It **might have been** better to work in smaller groups.*

Exercises

1 Write the verbs in the correct form to create conditional type 3 sentences.

1 If we (launch)________ the product sooner, we (beat) __________ the competition. But we didn't beat them.

2 Sorry this work is late. I (complete) __________ it on time if my computer (not crash) _________.

3 You need to improve customer service. You (not /lose) ________ those customers if you (offer) ________ them better service.

4 He's disappointed that he didn't get the promotion. He (be /promoted) __________ if he (have) _________ better qualifications.

5 They're having a lot of problems with that equipment. If they (listen)________ to my advice, they (invest) ___________ in better equipment.

6 If they (buy) __________ the more expensive model, it (last) __________ longer.

2 Write the verbs with a suitable past modal form to complete the sentences with the meaning that is given in brackets.

1 We (not find) _____________ the solution without your expert help. (praise)

2 You (tell) __________ me you had changed the time of the meeting. (criticism)

3 It (be) ________ better to postpone it till the next day. (alternative possibility)

4 They (not /give) __________ out that information – it was confidential. (criticism)

5 Why did you spend so much money? You (get) _________ a better deal from the other supplier. (alternative possibility)

Key to Exercise 1

1 had launched – would have beaten
2 would have completed – hadn't crashed
3 wouldn't have lost – had offered
4 would have been promoted – had had
5 had listened – would have invested
6 had bought – would have lasted

Key to Exercise 2

1 couldn't / wouldn't have found
2 should have told
3 might have been
4 shouldn't have given
5 could / might have got

Passives

Passives are more common in formal English, especially in written reports and formal minutes. There are three types of passive.

- direct passive

  Subject + passive verb

  The problem ***is*** *currently* ***being investigated.***

  A copy of the report ***has been circulated.***

  The equipment ***will be installed*** *next week.*

- indirect passive

  Indirect object + passive verb + direct object

  We ***weren't told*** *about the budget cuts.*

  The MD ***will be sent*** *a summary of the report.*

  He ***was given*** *three months' notice.*

- *it*-constructions

  it + passive verb + *that* clause

  It ***was agreed that*** *the new procedures would be implemented as soon as possible.*

  It ***was decided that*** *the whole team should be invited.*

Modals in the passive

Modal verb + *be* + past participle

Customers ***should be*** *listed by region.*

Passives have the following uses.

- When the agent is unknown or unimportant

  The product ***has been*** *thoroughly* ***tested.***

  The new model ***will be launched*** *next week.*

  The conference ***is scheduled*** *for 9th April.*

- systems and processes

  Forms ***should be handed*** *in by Friday.*

  Requests for payment ***are approved*** *by the head of department.*

- avoid personalising opinions or suggestions in minutes and reports

  It ***was*** *generally* ***felt*** *that the product needed a new image.*

  It ***was proposed*** *that a new offer should be made.*

- reporting unconfirmed information

  The CEO ***is said to be*** *in favour of the new warehouse.*

  He ***is expected*** *to make a decision next week.*

Exercises

1 Rewrite the sentences below in the passive. Start your passive sentence with the phrase given. Omit the person(s) if they are not necessary to the meaning.

1 Jenny circulated copies of the report to all staff.

2 You should submit all expense claims by the end of the month.

3 The finance department has to approve claims before they can make reimbursement.

4 Lots of people feel that the new system is unfair.

5 We don't expect the suppliers to lower their price.

2 Rewrite these sentences from the minutes using the passive form.

Project team meeting, July 18th, 10:00

1 We received apologies from Ann Hudson.

2 We approved the minutes of the last meeting.

Point 1: Abidjan project

3 We discussed the advantages and disadvantages of accepting the project.

4 We agreed that the project would be good for the company's reputation.

5 Patrick Lamarre pointed out that we could save costs by using local labour.

6 He has not carried out any detailed cost breakdown.

7 We agreed that we needed further research before going ahead.

Key to Exercise 1

1 have been circulated to all staff

2 should be submitted by end of the month

3 have to be approved before reimbursement can be made

4 is generally felt that the new system is unfair.

5 aren't expected to lower their price.

Key to Exercise 2

1 Apologies were received from Ann Hudson.

2 The minutes of the last meeting were approved.

3 The advantages and disadvantages of accepting the project were discussed.

4 It was agreed that the project would be good for the company's reputation

5 Patrick Lamarre pointed out that costs could be saved by using local labour

6 No detailed cost breakdown has been carried out.

7 It was agreed that further research was needed before going ahead.

Comparatives and superlatives

Comparatives are formed as follows.

- for one-syllable adjectives, add *-er*
  higher, lower, longer, tougher, stronger
  Telephone costs are ***lower*** *than they were 10 years ago.*
- adjectives ending in *y* change to *-ier*
  easier, prettier, heavier
  This model is ***easier*** *to use.*
- use *more* or *less* with multi-syllable adjectives
  more interesting, more convenient, less powerful
  The X100 is ***more economical*** *to run.*
- irregular comparative forms
  better, worse, further, farther
  Call me if you need any ***further*** *details.*
  The new offices are ***farther*** *from the city centre.*
- **Note**
  This model is ***bigger than*** *that one.*
  This model ***is the same price as*** *that one.*
  This model ***isn't as expensive as*** *that one.*

Superlatives are formed as follows.

- for one-syllable adjectives, add -est
  shortest, tallest, oldest, youngest
  She's the ***youngest*** *member of the team.*
- for adjectives ending in *y*, change to *-iest*
  easiest, prettiest, heaviest
  This model is ***the heaviest*** *of the three.*
- use the most / least for multi-syllable adjectives
  Camera phones are ***the most popular*** *nowadays.*
  This project was ***the least successful.***
- irregular superlative forms
  best, worst
  This phone has all ***the best*** *features.*
  This product is ***the worst*** *of the lot.*

Comparative and superlative adverbs

- add *more* / *less* for comparative adverbs
  Photos can be downloaded ***more quickly.***
- add the *most* / *least* for superlative adverbs
  It's our ***most successfully*** *marketed product.*
- irregular adverbs add *-er* / *-est*
  faster, fastest; harder, hardest; later, latest
  Her team worked ***faster*** *than ours.*

Exercises

1 Write the adjectives in the comparative form to complete the text.

Some online retailers are ([1] good) __________ than others. Online CD retailers usually have ([2] user-friendly) _________ websites and ([3] powerful) ________ facilities to help you find the CD you want. Generally, online prices are ([4] low) __________ than on the high street. Some retailers charge a lot for delivery, but it can still be ([5] cheap) __________ overall than buying from a store. When you buy online, there's a ([6] great) __________ chance that it won't be what you want. You have the right to return the goods, but some retailers are ([7] happy) __________ to take goods back than others.

2 Write the adjectives in the superlative form.

The TX is the model I recommend for our company car fleet. It offers the ([1] good) __________ value for money and is the ([2] economical) __________ to run. Of the models we looked at, we found this one to be the ([3] comfortable) __________ to drive over long distances. There is plenty of room, even for the ([4] tall) _________ drivers. It was also the ([5] easy) __________ to park. Consumer reports show that this model is the ([6] reliable) _________ car in its class.

3 Correct the mistakes in the following sentences.

1 You can buy an exercise bike for your home that is as good than the ones in the gym.
2 Expensive machines are usually more stronger.
3 You can adjust the speed to go more fast or more slowly.
4 It's better to train regularly for short periods as to spend too long on one session.
5 The worse thing you can do is to try to go too fast before you are really fit.
6 Exercising in front of the TV is least boring than going to the gym.

Key to Exercise 1
1 better 2 more user-friendly 3 more powerful
4 lower 5 cheaper 6 greater 7 happier

Key to Exercise 2
1 best 2 most economical 3 most comfortable
4 tallest 5 easiest 6 most reliable

Key to Exercise 3
1 as good as (not as good than) 2 stronger (not more stronger) 3 faster (not more fast) 4 better … than … (not as)
5 the worst (not worse)
6 less boring (not least)

The language of change

Adjectives have the following uses.

- before nouns

  There was a ***sharp*** *rise in profits last year.*

  We saw a ***sudden*** *increase in sales of smartphones.*
- after stative verbs such as *be, become, seem*

  The falling share price could be ***serious.***

  The market is becoming ***unstable.***

Adverbs have the following uses.

- after verbs

  Investment in computers rose ***sharply*** *in the 80s.*

  When giving presentations, it is important to speak ***slowly.***
- before an adjective, adverb or past participle

  This idea is ***extremely*** *risky.*

  The prices have been rising ***fairly*** *slowly.*

  They're all ***well****-qualified candidates.*
- irregular adverbs

  fast, hard, late, well

  The scandal hit the company ***hard.***

The language of change

- increase

  Verbs: rise, go up, grow, improve

  Nouns: increase, rise, growth, improvement, upturn
- decrease

  Verbs: fall, go down, drop, decline, deteriorate

  Nouns: decrease, fall, drop, decline, deterioration, downturn
- stability

  Verbs: to remain steady / constant / stable; to stay at the same level
- instability

  Verbs: fluctuate, vary, go up and down

  Adjectives: fluctuating, variable, unstable
- prepositions

  The chart shows an increase ***in*** *sales of ten per cent.*

  The total rose ***from*** *500* ***to*** *520 last month.*

  Sales have increased ***by*** *five per cent.*

  Profits fell ***to*** *a low point of €400m.*

  Tourist numbers reached a peak ***of*** *400,000.*

  The numbers remained steady ***at*** *30,000.*

  At the start of the year, the figure stood ***at*** *350.*

  The price fluctuated ***between*** *$20* ***and*** *$40 per unit.*

Exercises

1 Change the adjectives to adverbs where necessary.

Next year is expected to be a ([1]bad) _______year for car sales. During the 1990s, the industry grew ([2] marginal) ________ by 1.3 per cent per year. But since 1999, global volumes have seen a ([3] moderate) _______ fall. Demand for cars in new markets like China has risen ([4] dramatic) _________, but in the rest of the world, it has been ([5] flat) _______. The problem is that there are too many car manufacturers, and the situation is getting ([6] steady) _________ worse. The rising demand in ([7] fast) _______ growing markets like China will ([8] increasing) _______ be met by ([9] local) _______ firms and not by the ([10] big) __________ players such as Ford and Toyota.

2 Complete each gap with a suitable word.

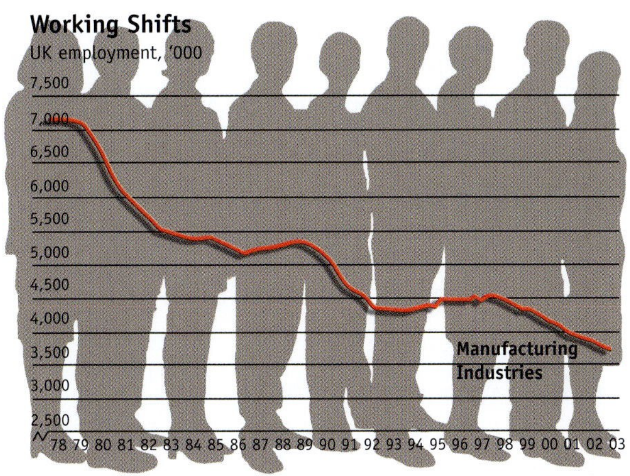

1 Jobs in manufacturing _________ sharply between 1980 and 1984.

2 During the mid-1980s, employment __________ steady at around 5.3m.

3 This was followed by another rapid ________ from 1990 to 1992.

4 During the mid-1990s, the numbers __________ slightly.

5 By 2003, the number had reached a _____ point of 3.75 million.

Key to Exercise 1

In change 2 marginally 3 no change 4 dramatically 5 no change 6 steadily 7 no change 8 increasing 9 no change 10 no change

Key to Exercise 2

1 fell / dropped / declined / decreased
2 remained 3 fall / drop / decline / decrease
4 rose / increased / went up / improved 5 low

Articles

The indefinite article is used with the following.

- non-specific singular count nouns

  I'm working on ***a*** *new project.*

  There's ***a*** *good course on management in May.*
- jobs and nouns of nationality

  I'm ***a*** *sales manager.*

  It's ***a*** *Dutch firm but the director is German.*

The definite article is used with the following.

- nouns already mentioned or specified

  The *results of* ***the*** *tests we've carried out aren't ready yet.*

  The *figures for the last quarter are now due.*
- nouns that are one of a kind, including titles

  the world, the internet, the CEO, the head of department, the HR department
- groups of people

  the Japanese, the unemployed, the wealthy, the staff
- superlative forms of adjectives

  We'll start with ***the most important point.***

  Please reply by Friday at ***the latest.***

No article is needed with the following.

- proper names

  Our head office is in ***Hamburg.***

  He works for ***Apple Computer*** *in California.*
- general plural and uncountable nouns

  People *are sending more and more emails.*

  It's important that ***objectives*** *are achievable.*

  How's ***business*** *these days?*
- some abstract nouns

  Different cultures have different attitudes to ***time.***

  Courtesy *is essential in business.*

  Do you work in ***finance****?*
- some prepositional phrases

  at home, at work, at university, by train

  She's studying ***at university.***

Exercises

1 Complete the letter, using *a / an*, *the*, or no article.

Dear Sirs

Re: Vacant post at 1 _____ Office of Fair Trading

I am writing to apply for 2 ____ post of Case Officer, as advertised in 3 ___ Economist on 4 ___ 7th February.

As you can see from 5 ___ attached CV, I am 6 ____ Dutch national with 7 ___ Masters Degree in Economics from 8 ____ University of Rotterdam. Since graduating, I have been working for 9 ___ McAllisters, 10 ____ investment bank in London, where I am in charge of 11 ____ project management team. 12 ___ goal of our team is to help 13 ____ companies to achieve 14 ___ successful mergers. I believe this experience has given me 15 ___ valuable experience in ...

2 Complete the article, using *a / an*, *the*, or no article.

Hollywood has learned to love the DVD.

For most of 1 ___ people who run Hollywood, 2 ___ romance of film is linked to 3 ___ movie theatres and 4 ___ movie stars. But nowadays, 5 ___ great many people watch films at 6 ___ home. Thanks to 7 ___ DVD, and its ability to store 8 ___ three-hour movie with 9 ___ high quality on 10 ___ small disc, Hollywood now earns more money from 11 ___ home entertainment than from 12 ___ showing of films in 13 ____ cinemas.

Key to Exercise 1

1 the 2 the 3 The 4 — 5 the 6 a 7 a 8 the 9 —
10 an 11 a 12 The 13 — 14 — 15 —

Key to Exercise 2

1 the 2 the 3 — 4 — 5 a 6 — 7 the 8 a 9 —
10 a 11 — 12 the 13 —

Linking sentences and ideas

Longer sentences have several parts: a main clause and one or more sub-clauses.

- linking words that come at the beginning of a sub-clause or a second main clause.

  Cause: *because, as, since, so that*

  Contrast: *but, although, while, whereas*

  We need a larger budget ***because*** *costs have increased.*

  Since *we now use electronic tags, counterfeiting is no longer a problem.*

  We must keep this secret ***so that*** *our competitors won't hear about it.*

  Although *there has been a growth in demand, our sales have not increased.*

- words and phrases that link ideas but can appear at the start, in the middle or at the end:

  Consequence: *therefore, consequently, as a result*

  Contrast: *however, on the other hand*

  Additional information: *what's more, in addition, furthermore*

  We need to stay ahead of the competition. It is very important, ***therefore****, to update our products.*

  We need to spend more. We shouldn't spend too much, ***however****.*

- phrases that are followed by a noun: *due to, because of, as a result of*

  As a result of *the increase in internet crime, many companies are raising their security budget.*

Relative clauses

- defining relative clauses define or differentiate the person or thing they refer to.
- the relative pronoun must be used when it is the subject of the verb that follows.

  People ***who*** *travel on business are very demanding customers.*

  It was the total ***that*** *was most disappointing.*

  the competitors ***whose*** *products are most similar to ours have also lost sales this year.*

- The relative pronoun can be omitted if it is the object of the verb that follows.

  The figures ***(that)*** *we recorded were unusually high.*

  The customers ***(whom)*** *we visited in Turin were all very interested.*

- non-defining relative clauses only give extra information and do not define what they refer to.

  Sales were below the target, ***which*** *was disappointing.*

Exercises

1 Complete the text about the fast food industry with suitable linking words or phrases.

Fast food is generally bad for you [1]_______ it is fried in unhealthy oils. [2] ______ the high cost of healthier oils, most restaurants are reluctant to change. A restaurant uses about 1,000 litres of oil a week; [3] _____, switching to a more expensive oil would cost $19,000 a year.

Salads are not always healthier: a chicken salad with dressing may contain 50 gm of fat, [4] _____ a single burger contains only 25 gm.

The main problem, [5]_____, lies with the consumer: only five per cent of customers order salads as a main meal. [6] _______, this figure is decreasing, not increasing.

2 Complete the sentences below with an appropriate relative pronoun. In some sentences, no pronoun is needed.

1 John Browne, ______ heads BP, Europe's largest oil company, is keen to reduce greenhouse gases.

2 One country ______ is becoming more important as a global oil producer is Russia.

3 China, ________ economy has been growing at eight per cent a year, accounts for a third of the world's growth in oil demand.

4 Many African countries are now exporting oil, ____ is helping to promote their economic growth.

5 An article ________ we read in The Economist reports that Nigeria is the biggest African oil producer.

6 A man _______ I met at a conference recently thinks that global oil demand will decrease.

Key to Exercise 1

1 because 2 Due to / Because of / As a result of
3 therefore / consequently / as a result
4 while / whereas, 5 however
6 What's more / Furthermore

Key to Exercise 2

1 who 2 that 3 whose 4 which 5 (that) – omit
6 (whom) – omit

Gerunds and infinitives

Gerunds have the following uses.

- after some prepositions: *before, after, without*
  Let's discuss that ***after watching*** *the video.*
- after some verb + prepositional phrases
  I'm not interested in ***paying*** *extra for insurance.*
  We apologise for ***keeping*** *you waiting.*
- as a noun
  Taking *time to think is always a good strategy.*
- after certain expressions: *it's no use, it's no good, have difficulty, be used to, look forward to*
  It's no use ***worrying*** *about it.*
  We're looking forward to ***meeting*** *you.*
- after certain verbs: *consider, delay, dislike, finish, involve, postpone, practise, report, risk*
  We've just finished ***drawing up*** *the contract.*
- in some suggestions
  How about / what about ***having*** *lunch?*
  I suggest / recommend ***travelling*** *first class.*
  Try ***phoning*** *after 6 pm.*

Infinitives have the following uses.

- stating purpose
  Our main objective is ***to make*** *more profit.*
  Our goal is ***to develop*** *better relations.*
  The first reason is ***to increase*** *productivity.*
- with adjectives
  Our website is very easy ***to navigate.***
  It's important ***to have*** *delivery by Friday.*
- after certain verbs: *afford, agree, aim, arrange, decide, expect, fail, hope, intend, manage, need, offer, plan, promise, refuse, want*
  They've offered ***to reduce*** *the price.*
- after certain verbs + object: *advise, allow, ask, cause, enable, help, invite, permit, persuade, remind, tell, warn*
  We asked you ***to quote*** *for the whole project.*
- the verbs *like* and *prefer* can be followed by either a gerund or an infinitive with no difference in meaning.
- some verbs can be followed by either a gerund or an infinitive, but with a difference in meaning.
  He ***stopped*** *to answer the phone. He* ***stopped*** *smoking.*
  Remember *to phone me! He doesn't* ***remember*** *phoning me.*

Exercises

1 Complete the dialogue by writing the verbs in either a gerund or infinitive form.

Mel You asked us (1 quote) ________ for a comprehensive IT service contract, and I think we've given you a reasonable proposal. Now you're saying that you're not interested in (2 sign) _______ a contract for full service cover.

Bob Our objective is (3 make sure) _______ that we have adequate support but without (4 make) _____ a full commitment to one service supplier. (5 work)_______ with two or three different suppliers will enable us (6 draw) ______ on the different skills and abilities that each company has to offer.

Mel You don't want (7 make) _________ a commitment, but you're expecting us (8 make) _____ one.

Bob We're offering (9 pay) ______ you for partial support. It's still a good deal for you. How about (10 give) ________ it your consideration, at least?

2 Complete the article by writing the verbs in either a gerund or infinitive form.

How to save money in an economic downturn

The symbol of bad economic times is the dying office plant. Companies stop (1 water) _______ their plants when they can't afford (2 pay) _______ someone to do the job. When budgets get better, they start (3 water) ________ again – and even think about (4 buy) ______ more plants.

Another symbol is company (5 train) _______. In good times, companies spend more on (6 train) _______, and especially on (7 provide) ________ development programmes for junior staff. At the same time, senior managers can look forward to (8 go) ________ off on conferences abroad.

In good times as well as in bad, the big leaders are used to (9 pay) _________ themselves huge sums of money. This is something that is not expected (10 change) _________ in the near future.

Key to Exercise 1
1 to quote 2 signing 3 to make sure 4 making
5 Working 6 to draw 7 to make 8 to make
9 to pay 10 giving

Key to Exercise2
1 watering 2 to pay 3 watering /to water
4 buying 5 training 6 training 7 providing
8 going 9 paying 10 to change

Reported speech

Speech can be reported using the same words as the speaker used.

- with the same tense

  He says he never goes to meetings.

  Phil says he can persuade the suppliers to reduce their price.

- **changing the tense to the past (especially in minutes of meetings)**

  *Jane reported that her team **had** problems with the new procedures.*

  *Harri commented that the report **contained** a lot of errors.*

  Note these changes to modal verbs in reported speech:

  must changes to *had to*

  will changes to *would*

  can changes to *could*

  may changes to *might*

  *Carlo expressed concern that sales **might** drop next year.*

Speech can be reported by summarising what a speaker said rather than using the same words.

Jacques stressed the importance of good design.

Gina raised the question of reliability.

- reporting verbs + *that* clause: *agree, believe, express the opinion, estimate, feel, point out, report, say, stress, suggest*

  Everyone agreed that more training was needed.

  Mr Jackson pointed out that local labour would be expensive.

  It was felt that too much time was wasted in travelling.

- reporting verbs + infinitive:

  agree, decide, offer, promise, refuse

  We've agreed to hold monthly meetings.

  Hannah has promised to keep everyone informed.

- reporting verbs + object + infinitive: *ask, tell, warn*

  The board has asked us to report back with our comments.

  The technical department warned us to use the safety procedures.

- reporting verbs + gerund:

  admit, consider, deny, discuss, suggest, talk about

  We've considered postponing the project.

  Tina suggested mailing all customers.

Exercises

1 Below are some of the things that different people have said about getting into a conference. Report the first two sentences using 'She says ...'

1 Everyone has to wear an identity badge.
2 Door staff will check all the badges.

Report the next four using 'He said that ...'

3 You must have a badge if you want to enter the conference.
4 You can collect your badge from reception desk.
5 Some unauthorised people may try to get in.

2 Summarise what the speakers said using the reporting verbs given.

1 'How about advertising on local radio?'
Sara suggested ____________________.
2 'There isn't enough time to do detailed research.'
Henry pointed out that ____________________.
3 'OK, let's set the launch date for January 4th.'
They all agreed ____________________.
4 'Please go ahead and make all the arrangements.'
The planning group was told ______________.
5 'When is the deadline for the feasibility report?'
George raised the question ________________.

Key to Exercise 1

1 She says everyone has to wear an identity badge.
2 She says doorstaff will check all the badges.
3 He said that you had to have a badge if you wanted to enter.
4 He said that you could collect your badge from the reception desk.
5 He said that some unauthorised people might try to get in.

Key to Exercise 2

1 Sara suggested advertising on local radio.
2 Henry pointed out that there wasn't enough time to do detailed research./pointed out the lack of time for detailed research.
3 They all agreed to set the launch date for January 4th / agreed on January 4th for the launch date
4 The planning group was told to go ahead and make the arrangements
5 George raised the question of the deadline for the feasibility report.

Pairwork

Unit 2 Task 2 Page 12

Role A: Andy

Look at your plan for tomorrow. You want to leave at 16:00 for a doctor's appointment.

Find someone who can work with the new trainee in your place.

THURSDAY 8

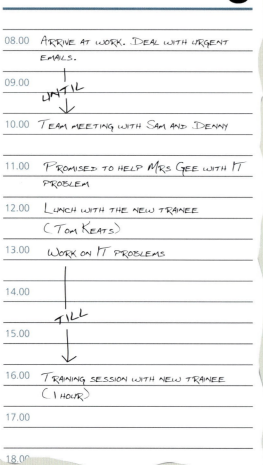

08.00	Arrive at work. Deal with urgent emails.
09.00	↓ until ↓
10.00	Team meeting with Sam and Denny
11.00	Promised to help Mrs Gee with IT problem
12.00	Lunch with the new trainee (Tom Keats)
13.00	Work on IT problems
14.00	↓
15.00	till ↓
16.00	Training session with new trainee (1 hour)
17.00	
18.00	

Unit 4 Task 2 Page 38

Role A

You want to spend the money on a special celebration. Suggest a dinner and night at an expensive hotel in (city of your choice). You want to invite wives / husbands / partners to the event.

Unit 5 Task 2 Page 26

Problem: Alex's Brief:

It's 8:00 and you should be on the plane by now. But there has been a problem with the computer system at the airport. It means that nobody can check in for their flights. There are long queues of people waiting at the check-in desk. The situation is very chaotic. There's no information about what's going to happen. You don't know how long you will be delayed. You don't even know if you'll be able to travel today!

Phone your partner in Barcelona and explain the problem. You don't have to take any decision. End by saying you'll call back when you have more information.

Unit 12 Task 3 Page 59

Role A: You are in favour of the proposal.

Arguments:

- It is becoming more and more difficult to compete in international markets.
- The pay for workers in developing countries is about one tenth of the average UK pay. Employment law is more relaxed, so it's easier to ask workers to work longer hours.
- The company will save around €100,000 a year in labour costs.
- You will be able to increase productivity.
- You will be much more profitable and more competitive.

Unit 9 Task 1 Partner A

Conversation topics

Summer holidays
Films
Gifts
Smoking
Food

Unit 14 Task 3 Page 69

Role A:

You prefer Site A. Use this information to answer your partner's questions. If you can't find the answer here, you'll have to say you don't know.

- Close to residential areas with some unemployment. Local workers easily available.
- Small possibility of some toxic materials on site: the site has been inspected and approved for re-development.
- There is a high crime rate in the area: need for strong security.
- The government has plans to re-develop and improve the area.
- Cost of transport to and from factory will be cheaper; cost of deliveries to customers same from both sites.

Unit 11 Task 3 Page 55

Role A: Bookings Manager

You have discovered that you made an error in the booking. You have booked two companies into the same room on the same day. The other company booked first, so Butternut will have to change their booking. You have two other rooms available but they are smaller. One holds 25 people, the other 15 people. You don't want to lose Butternut's business, so you need to find a suitable alternative solution for them. Your boss may not be happy if you have to offer compensation.

You can propose:

- The room for 30 people on another date (according to availability)
- One of the smaller rooms at a small discount
- Use of both smaller rooms for the price of one room
- A full refund plus a small discount off their next booking.

Unit 10 Task 2 Page 49

Dervla O'Connor

I'd like to propose an **increase** in the budget of **15** per cent. That may seem a **lot**, but there are **two** very good **reasons** why we need this increase.

Firstly because **online** sales are increasingly **important** to us. More than **55 per cent** of our customers buy via the **internet**, and this figure is **growing** every **year**. But people **won't** buy online if they are worried about the **risks**. So we **must** make sure that our systems are **trustworthy**.

Secondly because of internet **crime**. Internet **criminals** are becoming more and more **sophisticated**. So we need to **increase** our efforts in order to stay **ahead**. That means **increasing** what we spend on **up-dating** and **improving** our systems.

The internet offers enormous **benefits** to us. If we want to make the **most** of this **potential**, we must develop the **best possible** security systems. **That's why** I'm proposing a **substantial** increase in the security **budget**.

Unit 2 Task 2 Page 12

Role B: Bill

Look at your plan for tomorrow. An important client wants to visit you between 12:00 and 14:00. Find someone who can take the Irish group to lunch in your place.

THURSDAY 8

08.00
08:30 (?) Arrive back from New York
09.00 after overnight flight
10.00 (?) Get to the office
11.00 Meeting with group from Irish subsidiary
12.00 Lunch with Irish group in Directors' restaurant
13.00
14.00 Show the group round
15.00 Continue the meeting
16.00
16:30 (?) Go home and get some sleep
17.00 (I hope!)
18.00

Unit 4 Task 2 Page 23

Role B

You are going to open the meeting. You think the money should be given in the form of shares in the company (stock options).

Unit 5 Task 3 Page 27

Problem 2: Eddy's Brief

Your name is Eddy and you work in the transport department in the same company as Charlie. You've just received a phone call from the driver of a van delivering an urgent consignment to Makers Ltd. The van has had an accident. Due to icy conditions on the road, it skidded out of control and hit a tree. The driver is unhurt but the van is badly damaged. It is about 100 km from the delivery destination. You don't know if the consignment has been damaged in the accident

Unit 12 Task 3 Page 59

Role B: You are partly in favour of the proposal.

You think the manufacture of some basic devices (e.g. toasters) could be transferred abroad, but the production of newer, more innovative products should stay in the UK.

Arguments:

- Manufacturing of some products abroad will make the company more profitable and more competitive.
- The company could save around €60,000 a year in labour costs.

  Production of new products should remain in the UK because:
- It would be more difficult for designers to work closely with production teams when new product lines are being developed.
- It will save some UK jobs.

Unit 12 Task 3 Page 59

Role C: Bill

You are mainly against the proposal

You agree with the economic argument, but you think the move will bring bad publicity and damage the company's image.

Arguments:

- There is sure to be a lot of criticism in the press and on TV.
- Many people are concerned about the exploitation of workers in developing countries: that they are forced to work long hours in bad conditions, and for very low pay.
- There is a risk that consumers will boycott your products.

Unit 14 Task 3 Page 69

Role B:

You prefer Site B. Use this information to answer your partner's questions. If you can't find the answer here, you'll have to say you don't know.

- Currently the nearest residential area is five kilometres away.
- Permission has been given to develop the site, but some local people are against it.
- The area has a low crime rate.
- The government has plans to develop the surrounding area by building both offices and housing.
- Cost of transport to and from factory will be higher; cost of deliveries to customers same from both sites.

Unit 2 Task 3 Page 13

Use this form for your notes.

Action points		Deadline		Person responsible	
1		1		1	
2		2		2	
3		3		3	
4		4		4	
5		5		5	
6		6		6	

Unit 2 Task 2 Page 12

Role C: Sam

Look at your plan for tomorrow. You have to make an important phone call to Australia at 8 o'clock in the morning. Find someone who can welcome the new trainee in your place.

THURSDAY 8

08.00	Welcome the new trainee (Tom Keats) and brief him on the work.
09.00	
10.00	Team meeting with Andy and Denny: introduce Tom.
11.00	Prepare figures for budget meeting at 16.00
12.00	Take Tom to lunch (with Alex)
13.00	- 15:00 Training session with Tom
14.00	
15.00	BUDGET MEETING (*important meeting - may take 2 hours)
16.00	
17.00	
18.00	

Unit 4 Task 2 Page 23

Role C

You want to divide the cash among you so you can each spend it as you wish.

Unit 11 Task 3 Page 55

Role B: Sales Manager

There is a problem with your conference room booking at the hotel. Here are some points to consider in your discussion with the Bookings Manager:

- You don't want to change the date of the conference because this would disrupt everybody's schedules.
- You don't really want to find another venue as there isn't much time before next week.
- As the hotel has made a mistake, you feel strongly that they should offer reasonable financial compensation.
- Probably not all 30 delegates will attend. There are usually 4 or 5 people who can't make it.

Unit 4 Task 2 Page 23

Role D

You want to spend the money on a special training course that all of you would attend. It could be a course in marketing, negotiating or English.

Unit 9 Task 1 Partner B

Conversation topics

Keeping fit
Shopping
Hotels
The lottery
Learning English

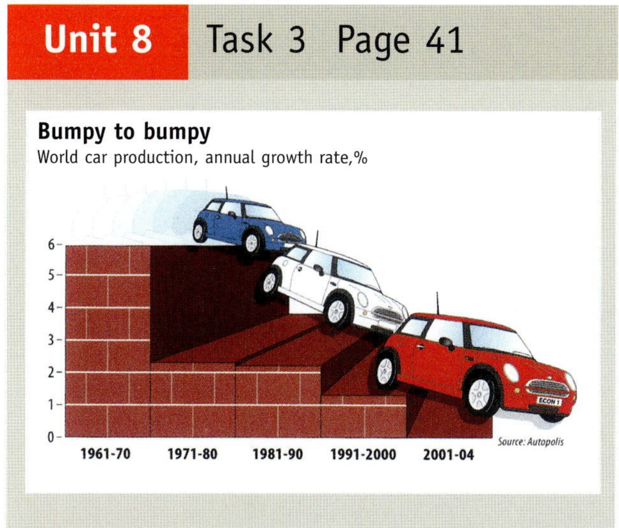
Unit 8 Task 3 Page 41
Bumpy to bumpy
World car production, annual growth rate,%
6
5
4
3
2
1
0
1961-70
1971-80
1981-90
1991-2000
2001-04
Source: Autopolis

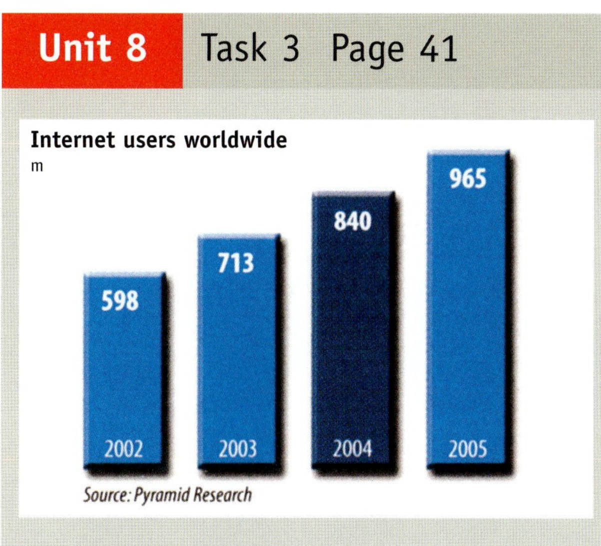
Unit 8 Task 3 Page 41
Internet users worldwide
m
598
2002
713
2003
840
2004
965
2005
Source: Pyramid Research

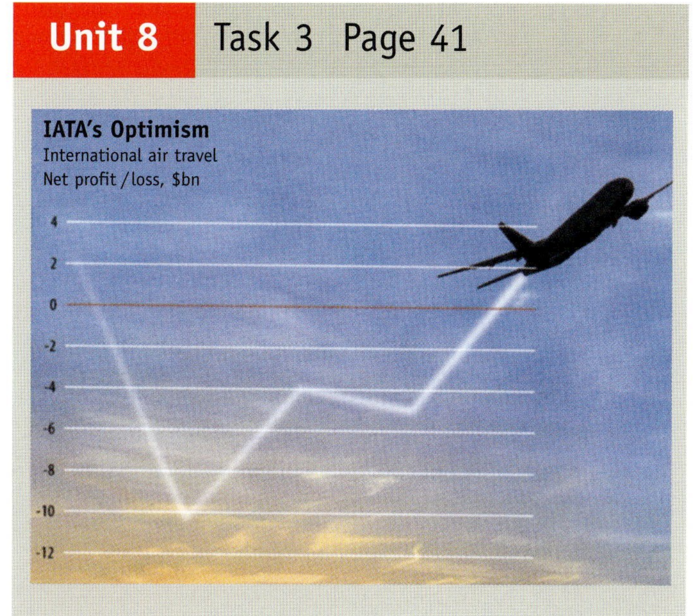
Unit 8 Task 3 Page 41
IATA's Optimism
International air travel
Net profit / loss, $bn
4
2
0
-2
-4
-6
-8
-10
-12

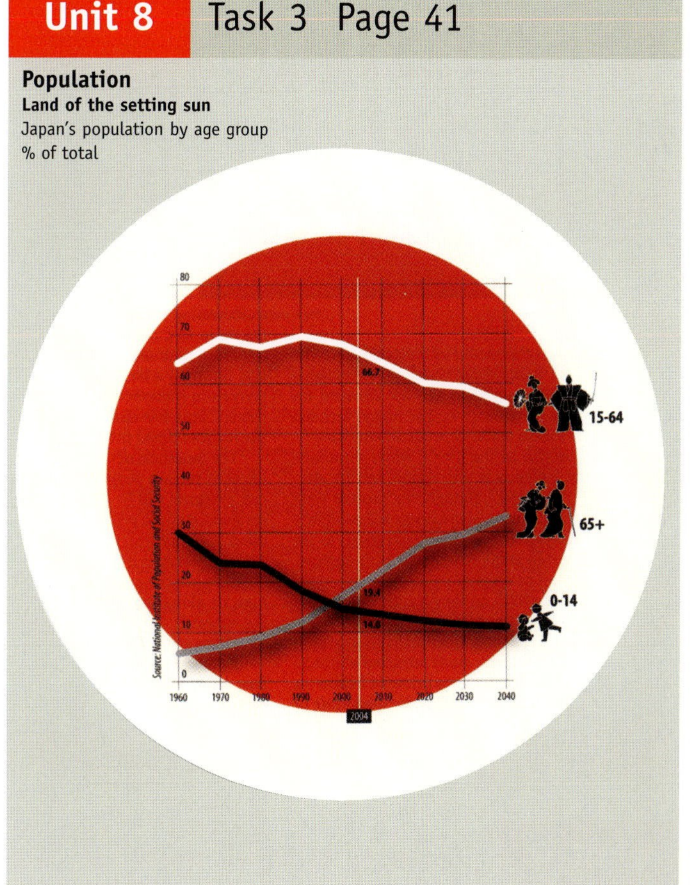
Unit 8 Task 3 Page 41
Population
Land of the setting sun
Japan's population by age group
% of total
15-64
65+
0-14
1960
1970
1980
1990
2000
2010
2020
2030
2040
2004

Unit 2 Task 2 Page 12

Role D: Denny

Look at your plan for tomorrow. The HR department has asked you to take part in a presentation to a group of graduates who want to join the company. The presentation is from 11:00 to 12:00. You have an appointment with a client at that time. Find someone else to take your part in the presentation.

THURSDAY 8

08.00	Take the children to school
09.00	Arrive at office – deal with emails
10.00	Team meeting with Andy and Sam.
11.00	Appointment with Jan Fix
12.00	Appointment with Petra Dax
13.00	Half hour lunch break 13.30 WORK ON PROPOSAL
14.00	
15.00	(** very important to finish and send it by 17.00!!!)
16.00	
17.00	
18.00	

Unit 4 Task 2 Page 23

Role E

You want to spend the money on a trip. Your company's head office is in New York and none of you has been there yet. Propose a visit.

Unit 12 Task 3 Page 59

Role D: You are completely against the proposal

Arguments:

- Thousands of UK workers will lose their jobs.
- The loss of jobs will have a bad effect on the local community
- The whole workforce will be angry about the move
- There is a risk that workers could go on strike
- If there was a long strike, this would cost the company a lot of money

Unit 11 Task 1 Page 52

Possible solutions to the $100 problem

Arguments:

1 One person takes $49.99, the other $50.01.
2 Add $10 ($5 each) to the total and then split it $55 each.
3 Take $49.50 each and give one dollar to charity.
4 Let fate decide – toss a coin.

Audioscripts

Unit 1 Listening page 8 (CD track 2)

Lisa: Good morning. I'm Lisa Guzman. Nice to meet you.

Paul: Paul Larousse. Nice to meet you, too.

Lisa: Sorry to keep you waiting – I had a long phone call from a customer.

Paul: Oh – no problem.

Lisa: Well, we have ten minutes before the meeting. Let's go up to my office. It's this way. [short pause] How was your trip?

Paul: It was fine – but a bit tiring.

Lisa: How long does it take from Canada?

Paul: Nine hours!

Lisa: That's a long time to be in a plane. I flew to Los Angeles last year. It took eleven hours! I was so bored ... Well – here we are. Please – have a seat.

Paul: Thanks.

Lisa: Would you like a cup of coffee – or tea?

Paul: Oh, no thank you. Perhaps a glass of water, if that's possible?

Lisa: Yes, of course. [short pause] Here you are.

Paul: Thanks.

Lisa: So how are things in Montreal? I hear you've got quite a big operation over there.

Paul: Yes. We're very busy at the moment. Sales are booming and we're expanding fast.

Lisa: How many people do you have?

Paul: Do you mean in the whole subsidiary? Three hundred and forty. But we're recruiting more people all the time. We expect to have about four hundred by the end of the year.

Lisa: That's really rapid growth. It must mean a lot of changes ...

Unit 2 Listening page 11 (CD track 3)

[SM = Sales Manager; CO = Conference Organiser]

SM OK. We've decided to organise a golf tournament for some of our most important customers. We're planning to hold the event in a luxury hotel with its own golf course. And we want to fix it for the 10th April – so we don't have much time.

CO Hmm. About nine weeks. Have you thought about which hotel?

SM Not yet. I wonder if you could phone round and get some details and prices? Get three or four so we can compare them and select the best one.

CO Of course, no problem.

SM Can we meet tomorrow morning and make a decision? This is urgent so we must do it right away.

CO Yes – tomorrow morning is fine with me.

SM We need to book as soon as possible.

CO Yes. Do you know how many people are coming?

SM Well, we won't know exactly until we invite the customers. We can tell the hotel it's for about 20 people, and we'll confirm the numbers later.

CO It's important to confirm the numbers quite soon. Let's say – by the end of February?

SM Fine. I'll tell the sales people to send out the invitations as soon as we decide on the hotel. Now – the food and drink arrangements ... We want to have lunch at the hotel, as well as coffee in the morning when the guests arrive, and cocktails and snacks at the end of the day. But before we choose the menu for lunch, we need to check if any guests have special requirements.

CO OK. I'd appreciate it if you could let me know the special requirements by the third week of March so I can agree the menu for lunch. I'd like to get everything done before April if possible.

SM I'll tell the sales staff and they'll contact you directly.

CO Thanks. Anything else?

SM Well, the last step is to brief the sales team on what's going to happen. But there's no rush – we can do that any time.

CO Perhaps in March or early April?

SM Yes, that's fine ...

Unit 3 Listening page 16

Part 1 (CD track 4)

Hello. My name's Leena Perttonen. I'm the marketing manager at AYT, and I'm going to give you a brief overview of our company. My aim is to outline the main reasons why you should consider AYT for your construction project.

First, I'll give you some general information about the company. Then I'll talk about our international operations. And finally, I'll point out the main reasons for our success.

So, let me start with the company.

Part 2 (CD track 5)

AYT was founded in 1912, and it's one of the oldest building companies in Finland. At first it was purely a construction company, building houses and apartment blocks in the residential construction sector. Now we are also a service company. We don't just build houses, we offer finance and maintenance services as well.

We are quite a big company with 22,000 employees. Last year we had a turnover of three billion euros, and made a net profit of more than 90 million euros. We are market leaders in Finland, with a 32 per cent share of the market. So you can see that we are a strong and successful company.

Well, that was some general information about the company. Now I'll move on to our international operations.

We have more than 40 years' experience of residential construction outside Finland. We have operations in Sweden, the Baltic States and Russia. In fact, more than a quarter of AYT employees work outside Finland. So we have a lot of experience in managing international construction projects.

And so to my final point: the reasons for our success.

Well, firstly, there's our expertise. We have chosen to specialise in building residential houses and apartments so we have excellent knowledge of this area.

Secondly, our quality standards are extremely high – as high as anywhere in the world. So we feel confident in offering long-term guarantees for all our work.

Thirdly, we have excellent project management and cost control. This is important so we can finish each project on time and in budget. It means that our clients don't have to worry about extra costs mounting up as a result of delays and poor planning.

So – to sum up. I hope to have shown you that we are a well-established company, financially sound and a market leader in the home market. We also have strong international experience in several countries outside Finland. We offer the highest possible standard of construction together with excellent project management. These are the reasons why you should consider AYT for your construction project.

Unit 4 Listening page 20 (CD track 6)

Director: Right – can we start? ... Good morning, everyone. Thanks for coming to this meeting. Do you all know Harriet Blofeld, my new personal assistant?

Harriet: Hello, everyone!

Director: Harriet will take the minutes of the meeting, if you all agree.

Director: Well – let me explain the background. As you know, we have created a new management model with a flatter hierarchy. Staff work in small project teams which are highly customer-focused. With no managerial positions, that means there are fewer prospects for promotion. We need to motivate staff by offering a different kind of reward. We've already decided to set up a performance-related pay system in which staff receive higher pay for achieving their targets. The question is: which method should we choose?

Specifically, we've got three objectives:

First, to examine the different reward schemes, to see how each one would work and to give you a chance to ask questions. Second, to decide on the most effective scheme for our company. And third, to prepare a proposal for the Board. Now we have to finish by 12 o'clock today, so the purpose of this morning's meeting is simply to look at the different options. We'll leave the decision till the next meeting.

Right. Now Joanna has done some research into performance-related reward schemes. Joanna, would you like to start by explaining the different options ... ?

Unit 5 Listening page 25 (CD track 7)

Dan: Hello, Dan McGuire.

Robert: Hello? Hello? – Is that Dan McGuire?

Robert: Hello, Dan. This is Robert.

Dan: Hi, Robert. How's it going? All ready to start construction today?

Robert: Well ... actually, no. I'm afraid we've got a problem. Some local farmers are protesting against the dam. They're saying they don't want to lose their farmland.

Dan: I can't believe it! I thought they agreed to this project. We paid them compensation, didn't we?

Robert: But now they say they don't agree. They're stopping the work from going ahead.

Dan: 'Stopping the work' – How do you mean exactly?

Robert: There are hundreds of people here. They're sitting on the ground where we want to start work, holding banners which say 'No to the dam' and 'This is our land'. Some people have tied themselves to our machines. I think there are some foreign activists among them – environmental groups from the US and from Europe.

Dan: Oh my! That's all we need! Couldn't we bring in some people to move them? What about the army?

Robert: I think it could be very dangerous. It might turn violent. Then some people would get hurt, and that would mean bad publicity for the company. Perhaps we could talk to them – offer them a bigger compensation package. These people are poor farmers – I'm sure they would be happy to get more money.

Dan: But what about the cost? We don't have any more money in the budget. And it'll mean lengthy negotiations. In fact, the longer the protest goes on, the longer we'll be delayed. We won't be able to finish on schedule and that'll result in even more expense!

Robert: What are we going to do?

Dan: Find out who's leading the protest. Talk to the leaders. Ask them why they changed their minds. I'm going to call a crisis meeting. I'll get back to you soon as I can.

Robert: OK, Dan. Bye.

Unit 6 Listening page 30 (CD track 8)

Lee Jones:

OK – you asked me to find out about international charges so that we can see which mobile phone service provider we should choose for our company.

So – let me show you these two charts. Chart A shows mobile phone calls to the UK from three other countries: Australia, Spain and the US. And chart B shows the cost of sending text messages from these countries.

As you can see, Orange offers the cheapest calls from both Spain and the US. But the important thing to notice is – Vodafone is *much* cheaper for calls from Australia. This is an advantage for us because Australia is our most frequent destination.

If you look at the cost of text messaging, you can see that O2 is the cheapest from Spain and the USA. But which is cheaper from Australia? Again Vodafone.

And Vodafone has another advantage. We can subscribe to their international traveller service for two pounds fifty per phone per month – that's in addition to the usual monthly tariff of course – and that means we can get a further reduction on all calls to and from the EU. So calls from Spain would cost only 60 pence – the same as with Orange. I've also talked to their sales people, and it seems we could probably negotiate a special deal on calls from the US as well.

So – to summarise. Orange is the cheapest overall for international mobile phone calls. But – Vodafone offers much cheaper calls from Australia. And if we subscribe to their international traveller service, we can get a discount on calls from Spain – and probably from the US as well.

So, in conclusion, I would recommend that we go with Vodafone.

Unit 7 Listening page 35

Extract 1 (CD track 9)

Leader (male): As you know, our profits have been poor in the last year. If we want to return to making good profit, we'll have to find a way to revive sales. So – any suggestions?

Director A: I think we should introduce more

discount sales. They always attract customers.

Leader: But that's not good for profits. Our margins are low enough already!

Director B: Perhaps we could close down the larger stores and relocate to smaller buildings in out of town locations.

Leader: Hmm – That could save a lot of costs! ...

Close down larger stores.

Director C: Maybe we could decorate our stores in a more modern style. That might bring in more people.

Leader: Yes, that's a good idea. Do you think we should have a more exciting image – more glitzy?

Director B: Hmm – I don't like glitz!

Extract 2 (CD track 10)

Leader: As you know, our profits have been poor in the last year. If we want to return to making good profit, we'll have to find a way to revive sales. So – any suggestions?

Director A: I think we should introduce more discount sales.

Leader: Right. Introduce more discount sales.

Director B (Bob): That's crazy. If we sell at a discount we'll just lose money!

Leader: Bob, we're just collecting ideas at the moment. If we stopped to evaluate each idea, it would take too long – and people wouldn't be as creative. So it's better not to make judgments for now, OK? So – any other ideas?

Director C: Maybe we could decorate our stores in a more modern style.

Leader: Decorate the stores. OK – go on.

Director A: How about if we change the displays more often and make them more exciting!

Director B: Why don't we organise some special events sometimes?

Director C: Yes – What if we held some fashion shows and invited celebrities to come?

Leader: OK, OK – give me time to write ...

Unit 8 **Listening** page 39 (CD track 11)

Listening 1

Example A

Hello! I've got some very good news for you this morning. Profits are up! I expect you'd like to see the details. Right – so let me show you the performance figures for the last six months.

Example B

I know that many of you here today are thinking about investing in our company. And you would like to know if we are a profitable company or not. Well, this morning, I'm going to present some figures which I hope will give you a picture of our performance over the last six months. I think you'll find them interesting.

Example C

How many people here have read *The Economist* this week? Have you seen the article about the technology market? Yes – at last, the technology market is starting to recover. And our company is part of that recovery. I'd like to tell you about the company's performance over the last six months, and you'll see that the figures are starting to look good!

Unit 8 **Listening** page 40 (CD track 12)

Listening 2

The handheld computer is **dead**, and the future is in **Smartphones**.

How do I **know**?

Just look at the **figures**.

As you can **see** – Sales of **PDAs** have stayed **flat** at around **eleven** million units **worldwide**.

What about sales of **Smartphones**?

They're rising **fast** from just **four** million **last** year to nearly **twelve** million **this** year.

The PDA **market** will never be a **mass** market.

Almost everyone who wants a **PDA** now **has** one.

Unit 9 **Listening** page 43

Conversation 1 (CD track 13)

Gerry: And can we have a bottle of mineral water, please? Sparkling. Thanks.

Serena: It's a lovely restaurant! It's so big, but it feels friendly somehow.

Gerry: Yes – In fact this building used to be a railway station.

Serena: Oh, really?

Gerry: This was the main hall where people bought their tickets. And if you look out the back, you can see where the old railway tracks used to be. That's now a shopping centre.

Serena: Yes, I can see ... It's a big development! Is it new?

Gerry: Not very new. I think this restaurant's been here about 20 years.

Serena: It's very popular, isn't it?

Gerry: Yes – but you should see it in the evening. Then it really comes alive! They often have live music here – mainly jazz – and people get up and dance. It has a very good atmosphere.

Serena: I can imagine!

Gerry: Do you like jazz?

Serena: Well – I don't know much about it really. I like traditional jazz – the old tunes. But I find modern jazz is a bit difficult to listen to. What about you?

Gerry: Oh – I love all kinds of jazz ...

Conversation 2 (CD track 14)

Paul: Well, it was a good meeting, Milo! I'm glad I came.

Milo: Yes. Very useful! Are you travelling back tonight?

Paul: Yes, my flight's at 7:00.

Milo: And when will you get home?

Paul: Well – probably not till ten or ten-thirty. The flight's about 90 minutes – then I have to pick up my car and it's another hour's drive from the airport. What about you? Do you have far to go?

Milo: I live about 30 kilometres from here. If there's no traffic I can do it in half an hour. But at this time of day ...

Paul: The rush hour!

Milo: Yes – it's terrible! It can take twice as long. But I don't usually leave the office till after six. Then the traffic's not so bad and I get home faster.

Paul: You're lucky! Where *I* live, the traffic's bad up to seven o'clock or even later. I'd have to work very late to avoid it.

Milo: Well – talking of bad traffic, we should order your taxi. It could take you an hour to get to the airport.

Paul: An hour!

Milo: Yes, really! On Friday the traffic can be particularly awful! Mia – Could you order a taxi for Paul – to go to the airport?

Mia: Yes, of course! I'll do it right away.

Milo: Well. if you'll excuse me, I'm going to leave you with Mia. I'm expecting a phone call from the States and I want to prepare myself for it.

Paul: Yes, of course.

Milo: It's been very good meeting you. Thanks very much for coming.

Paul: I'll email that information you wanted as soon as I'm back in the office tomorrow.

Milo: And we'll talk again very soon.

Paul: Yes. Thanks for everything.

Milo: Bye.

Paul: Bye.

Unit 10 Listening page 50 (CD track 15)

So why should we use **ID tags** to **identify** our **brand**? You **may** think that this is **unnecessary**. That it will simply **increase** the **cost** of manufacturing, and the **price** we charge to our **customers**. But there are a **number** of reasons why we need to take action **now** to protect our brand name.

The **first** reason **is** to reassure our **customers**. So that when people buy **our brand**, they can feel confident that it really **is** our brand, and **not** some cheap imitation. People expect a **high** standard of **excellence** from our products. So it's **very** important to regain customer **confidence**.

The **second** reason **is** to be able to **guarantee** our products. **Retailers** are obliged to refund the **cost** of faulty **fake** products which customers return to the **store**. Clearly, they wouldn't have sold the article if they'd **known** it wasn't **genuine**. So we want the retailers to **know** they are **fully** supported by our **guarantee**.

The **third** reason **is** that we want a **maximum** return on our **investment**. We've spent **millions** on development to get the product **right**. And we've spent millions **more** on **advertising** in order to build an image that **sells**. **Counterfeit** products have caused our sales to **drop**. At the same **time**, the counterfeiters are making a **profit** out of **our** ideas. This has to **stop**.

We have one of the **best-known** brands in the business. And if we **don't** take the threat of counterfeiting **seriously**, we'll **lose sales**. **ID tags** are an **effective** and **secure** method of protecting our **name** and our **investment**. **That's why** I'm proposing we invest in **ID tags**.

Now I'll hand over to Rosa to explain how the system works and what it's going to cost. Rosa ...

Unit 11 Listening page 53 (CD track 16)

Conversation 1

Viktor: Well – the thing is – we need to discuss the delivery terms. Up to now, we've always included free delivery in the price. But unfortunately, our transport costs have risen so much in the last few months that we're now going to have to charge for delivery.

Xavier: Pay for deliveries? There's no way! None of your competitors charge for deliveries!

Viktor: Not for the moment, no. But we think they'll have to take a similar step very soon. After all, their costs have risen just as much as ours!

Xavier: In the meantime, it's totally unacceptable. We'll have to switch to another supplier if you insist on this.

Conversation 2

Viktor: Well – the thing is – we need to discuss the delivery terms. Up to now, we've always included free delivery in the price. But unfortunately, our transport costs have risen so much in the last few months that we're now going to have to charge for delivery.

Yacoub: I see. Well, I can understand your position. But how much are you thinking of charging?

Viktor: We'd like to propose five per cent on each order.

Yacoub: Do you mean five per cent of the order value on each delivery?

Viktor: Yes, that's right.

Yacoub: Let me think ... Here's another idea. How about a flat rate of – say 20 euros per delivery? That way, we could save money by ordering less frequently and by ordering larger quantities. And you'd gain because you wouldn't have to deliver so often. And you could carry more in each load which would be economical.

Viktor: Hmm ... So you're saying you'd be willing to buy in larger quantities?

Yacoub: With the flat rate, we'd have the option to save money by doing that, yes.

Viktor: Well, it sounds like a reasonable idea ... But I'll need to do some calculations to see how it would work.

Unit 12 Listening page 57 (CD track 17)

Extract 1

Speaker A: Well, I'm in favour of the new recipe. There's so much bad publicity these days about the health risks of fatty foods. It's sure to discourage consumers from buying our products. And that's going to have a bad effect on our sales. I think we should make the change now before sales start to fall.

Speaker B: On the other hand, it might be better to wait and see. After all, we haven't seen any fall in sales so far.

Extract 2

Speaker A: The fact is – the trend is towards healthier food. More and more people are aware of the risks of overeating and becoming overweight. It's a trend we can't ignore.

Speaker C: I agree. And what's more, there's the risk of litigation. Remember there was a lawsuit in the States last year. The one where two overweight teenagers brought a case against one of our competitors ...

Extract 3

Speaker C: ... It could destroy us if we had to fight a lawsuit like that!

Speaker B: Can I just point out that so far no company has actually lost a lawsuit of that sort. Isn't it rather difficult to prove that just one food product made someone fat?

Extract 4

Speaker A: You have to remember, labelling is going to have to be more precise in future. Pressure groups are demanding it. We're going to have to say exactly how many grams of fat each pack contains. Our product is high in fat, and it simply won't ... look good ... if ...

Speaker B: Sorry to interrupt, but can I just ask: has anyone done any research into this? I mean – Do our customers actually read the labels? And if they do – will they know how many grams of fat is bad for them?

Extract 5

Speaker D: I have some figures here which say that the new recipe is going to cost more to produce. Surely we can't stay competitive in the market if our production costs go up?

Speaker A: Actually that's not quite right. It's true that the cost of the new ingredients is slightly higher. But there are ways that we can also save costs, for example, the cost of processing the new recipe is cheaper ...

Extract 6

Speaker A: ... We'll be able to buy in these ingredients ready prepared, so we can cut out part of our own production process. That means we'll need less space for production equipment and ...

Speaker D: Are you suggesting that we should cut jobs?

Speaker A: Just let me finish. I was going to say that we'll need less space for that product, so we can use it for expanding other lines. I don't think we'll need to cut any jobs, no.

Unit 13 Listening page 63 (CD track 18)

Extract 1

Leader: Well, at our meeting next July, we'll be together with our colleagues from the Southern Region. There'll be about 20 people instead of the usual ten. So we have to decide whether we can still hold the meeting here in the office or whether to hold it in a hotel. What do people think about this?

Leader: Peter, what do you think?

Extract 2

Peter: Well, I think it's a bad idea to hold the meeting in a hotel.

Leader: Right. Why do you think that?

Extract 3

Jenny: I don't think we have enough space here. We just have two small conference rooms. It isn't enough if we want to split into small groups to discuss things. We can't go to our offices, because the phone rings and we get distracted ...

Gaby: What about ... ?

Jenny: So we all have to fit into two small rooms for the whole time and I think it's going to be ...

Gaby: Can I just ... ?

Jenny: ... far too cramped, and with no chance to move around or ...

Gaby: I'd just like to say ...

Jenny: ... combine in different ways, so as to have a really productive meeting ...

Leader: OK! Thank you, Jenny. Gaby – you wanted to say something?

Extract 4

Frank: The issue concerning a hotel venue for our meeting is surely primarily one of financial disadvantage versus the adequacy of the office environment in affording good conditions for productivity. If the environmental factors cannot combine to foster an atmosphere conducive to creativity then I would suggest that the argument comes down in favour of making whatever financial outlay is required ...

Leader: Er – so what you are saying is that you are in favour of a hotel. Is that right?

Extract 5

Harry: Well I don't agree with the idea of a hotel. We all travel such a lot and spend most of our time staying in hotels. And I have to say – the expenses we get are never enough! I mean, we should be able to buy a drink in the bar in the evening without having to pay for it ourselves. I don't know why we can't get ...

Leader: Well, I don't think that belongs to the present discussion.

Extract 6

Leader: All right! Thank you for your views. So, to sum up, some of you are saying that a hotel environment is more stimulating, more likely to motivate people. Others think it's just an extra cost without any real benefits ...

Unit 14 Listening 1 page 66 (CD track 19)

Presenter: So to sum up ...

We've compared the case for building our own warehouse with our current practice of outsourcing distribution. We've looked at two main points: one, the cost; and two, efficiency in delivering to our customers. As we have seen, we'll break even on the investment in the warehouse in just five years. After that, we can expect to save costs on distribution. What's more, the warehouse will enable us to deliver faster and more efficiently to our customers.

My conclusion is, therefore, that the new warehouse should be built as soon as possible. Then we can have the benefits of greater **cost savings and** greater **efficiency** in the **future**.

Thank you for your attention.

Any questions?

Unit 14 Listening 2 page 67 (CD track 20)

Presenter: Thank you for your attention. Any questions? Yes?

Questioner 1: Building a warehouse is a big

investment. Can you please explain how we're going to manage it?

Presenter: Sorry – are you asking about financing?

Questioner 1: Financing, yes.

Presenter: Well – two banks have already agreed to lend us the capital we need. You can find the details in the handouts I gave you – er – page 14 ... The interest rates are very favourable.

Questioner 2: Surely it's too risky? What if there's a drop in sales? We won't be able to pay off the loans.

Presenter: That's a good question. But the sales forecasts are healthy and there's no reason why we should see a drop in sales. In fact, once the warehouse has been built, we should be able to expand, and that will give us greater stability.

Questioner 3: So what are the sales projections for the next five years?

Presenter: Er – I'm afraid I don't have that information here, but I can find out for you. Any other questions? Yes?

Questioner 4: You say that the cost of maintaining a warehouse would be low. Can you give us a full breakdown of running costs please?

Presenter: Sorry, I don't think we have time to go into that now, but we'll be discussing the details at our next meeting.

Daniel: Right. Is everyone happy with this decision?

All: Yes.

Daniel: Excellent. So what we've agreed is this. We'll manufacture the toy at our factory in Nantes. Jon – you'll supply the product

Unit 15 **Listening** page 72 (CD track 21)

specifications and all the design work. And you agree to be available at all times to act as consultant while setting up the production line. We've agreed to split the set-up costs fifty-fifty. Fabrox will be responsible for all operating costs. These costs will be paid back out of the sales income. We've agreed to split the profits 70 to 30. That's 70 per cent to Fabrox, 30 per cent to Jon. This agreement will be finalised in writing and signed by both parties at our meeting next week. Jon, we'll get a copy to you by courier before then.

Jon: Thanks. That sounds really good. I'd just like to say that I'm really pleased we've got a deal, and I think this venture is going to be a great success for both of us.

All: Hear! Hear!

Daniel: We're very pleased to be working with you. And I'm sure we're going to have a long and profitable relationship!

All: [Murmurs of agreement.]

Daniel: And now I think it's time to celebrate. We've booked a private room at the Gala restaurant and I believe they're keeping a few bottles of champagne on ice for us.

Jon: So what are we waiting for?

Daniel: Let's go!